P9-DMP-632

The
NECESSITY
of
STRANGERS

The
NECESSITY
of
STRANGERS

The Intriguing Truth About Insight, Innovation, and Success

Alan S. Gregerman

JB JOSSEY-BASS™
A Wiley Brand

Cover design: Adrian Morgan

Cover art: © Thinkstock

Published by Jossey-Bass
A Wiley Brand
One Montgomery Street, Suite 1200, San Francisco, CA 94104-4594—www.josseybass.com

Jossey-Bass books and products are available through most bookstores. To contact Jossey-Bass directly call our Customer Care Department within the U.S. at 800-956-7739, outside the U.S. at 317-572-3986, or fax 317-572-4002.

Wiley publishes in a variety of print and electronic formats and by print-on-demand. Some material included with standard print versions of this book may not be included in e-books or in print-on-demand. If this book refers to media such as a CD or DVD that is not included in the version you purchased, you may download this material at http://booksupport.wiley.com. For more information about Wiley products, visit www.wiley.com.

Library of Congress Cataloging-in-Publication Data
Gregerman, Alan S.
  The necessity of strangers: the intriguing truth about insight, innovation, and success/ Alan Gregerman. — First edition.
pages cm
Includes index.
    ISBN 978-1-118-46130-3 (hardback), 978-1-118-53459-5 (pdf), 978-1-118-53455-7 (epub)
  1. Creative ability. 2. Inspiration. 3. Technological innovations. I. Title.
  BF408.G673 2013
  650.1—dc23

                                                                              2013020945

Printed in the United States of America
FIRST EDITION

HB Printing   10 9 8 7 6 5 4 3 2 1

CONTENTS

PART THREE
Possibilities

To Lisa—my life's most enchanting stranger.

To Sara, Carly, and Noah—whose eyes make
my world more complete each day.

And to a world of strangers I've yet to
meet and learn from.

The only true voyage of discovery would not be to visit strange lands but to possess other eyes, to behold the universe through the eyes of another, of a hundred others, to behold the hundred universes that each of them holds, that each of them is.
—Marcel Proust

If you were asked to make a list of the most important reasons why leading companies and organizations are so successful, what would you come up with? If you are like many people, including leading business thinkers like Peter Drucker, Jim Collins, and Tom Peters, you would probably say that it has a lot to do with having

- *Visionary and effective leadership*
- *A clear and compelling purpose and strategy*
- *Great offerings tied to a powerful and unique value proposition*
- *The right people*
- *Real teamwork and collaboration*
- *The right knowledge*
- *A keen focus on the needs of customers*
- *A bit of luck*

You might also add award-winning quality to the mix, along with the right systems and processes, and cutting-edge or at least the most appropriate technology. If you had been exposed to enough TV commercials and ads for UPS, the giant parcel delivery company, you might even include logistics—the glue that holds everything together.

And if I were to ask you about the most important reasons why some people are so successful in their personal, social, and civic lives, you and many experts would probably come up with a relatively similar list. But you probably wouldn't include *strangers*. And why should you include people you have never met before and are not likely to go out of your way to meet? It's hard enough to get important things done by ourselves or with the help of people we know, understand, and trust, without having to worry about involving people we simply don't know. So strangers rarely figure in our thinking about business or personal success.

Now I'm here to tell you that they should. Or, better yet, to lead you on a journey to discover why strangers are the real key to our growth as individuals, companies, and organizations; to help you understand why they are our best secret weapon or greatest competitive advantage in the battle to innovate, create, and deliver greater value, and make a powerful difference in whatever we choose to do; to convince you, or have you convince yourself, that you will never reach your full potential—or even come close—by simply hanging out with the people you know or, more specifically, people who are a lot like you.

You just won't.

Not that friends, relatives, and colleagues aren't very important. Not that there is anything wrong with people who are a lot like you. They're just not enough. And in some ways they aren't helpful at all.

Your ability to engage, learn from, and collaborate with strangers who are very different from you—in terms of what they know and how they approach the world—is the real key to creating the remarkable breakthroughs that you are capable of, growing the enterprises you were meant to grow, finding and delighting the new customers you were meant to serve, and making the most of your own life. The exciting news is that you have the ability to unlock the real potential in strangers and the real potential in yourself, and all it will take is a sense of curiosity, a spirit of openness, a willingness to connect, and a pair of comfortable shoes.

Keep reading, and I will show you how to make it happen in clear, practical, and hopefully inspiring ways.

The Necessity of Strangers is organized into three parts. In the first part we'll look closely at the promise of strangers, the reasons for our innate aversion to them, and the keys to creating a more open mindset.

In Part Two we'll explore the five important areas of business and life in which strangers are essential to greater success:

1. *Innovation*: creating powerful new ways of doing the things that matter most by combining what we know best with the ideas and insights of strangers
2. *People*: figuring out how to engage and bring out the very best in ourselves and the strangers we hire
3. *Collaboration*: understanding how to leverage the full abilities of all of the strangers we could work and partner with
4. *Customers*: thinking about how we can grow our enterprises or any initiative by connecting with and learning from the right strangers
5. *Leadership*: learning how to lead in a world filled with strangers and limitless possibilities

Then, in the third part, I'll provide a set of tools that you can use today to unlock the power of strangers in your work and life, and I'll show you how travel to places near and far can be the spark to greater openness, possibilities, and success.

So thank you for being here and being open to the possibility that all of us and the companies and organizations we work in can become even more remarkable than we ever imagined by becoming more open to the ideas, insights, perspectives, and magic of strangers.

Alan Gregerman
Silver Spring, Maryland
2013

The
NECESSITY
of
STRANGERS

PART ONE

Frameworks

ONE

Necessity

It is better to walk than to curse the road.
—AFRICAN PROVERB

On a beautiful fall morning in 2006, a walk to the school bus with our daughter Carly—who was nine at the time—would challenge my thinking about life and the real keys to personal and business success. It was a walk that my wife or I made almost every school day, but on this particular morning, Carly and I would pass someone we'd never seen in our neighborhood before—a middle-aged gentleman who looked more than slightly disheveled, somewhat distraught, and, from my overly protective parental perspective, potentially dangerous. So once we were out of listening distance, I turned to Carly and said: "You know sweetheart, Mamma and Papa won't always be able to walk you to the school bus. So we'd like you to promise us that when you are walking by yourself you won't talk to strangers." It seemed like an important and necessary thing to say, especially at that moment. And it was something my parents had told me when I was Carly's age at a time when the world was a whole lot safer.

Yet I could never have imagined her response as she looked up at me and said: "But Papa, if I don't talk to strangers, how will I ever make new friends? And how will I ever learn new things?"

Her simple words would quickly challenge me to recall all of the "strangers" who had changed my life in some meaningful way.

Like Mrs. Marshall, my kind and encouraging kindergarten teacher at Heights Elementary School in Sharon, Massachusetts. She would set the tone for my love of learning from the moment we met by letting me know that it was perfectly okay to be a slow reader and by teaching me the importance of getting along with other people, even when they were exceedingly different—in other words, girls.

Or like Bill Ihlanfeldt, dean of admissions at Northwestern University in the 1970s. After interviewing me over a bowl of buffalo stew at Tommy's Joynt in San Francisco, he would send me a handwritten acceptance letter to a college that was clearly a stretch for a young man who was working as a subway mechanic, volunteering at a nursing home, and spending a lot more time playing basketball and repairing his car than studying to retake the SATs. Bill would end up checking my transcripts every quarter for four years and following up with handwritten notes of encouragement that continued unabated until I graduated summa cum laude—forcing me to learn the meaning of these three words and, as a result, double my knowledge of Latin.

Or my very first customers at GTE (now part of Verizon), First Union Bank (now part of Wells Fargo), and the NutraSweet Company. They would take a big chance on my brand-new business and our unique ideas for unlocking the genius and innovation in all of their people at a time when they could have chosen the "safer" path of working with a much larger and more established partner. I'm proud and humbled to report that each would say they made a wise business decision.

Or Lisa Otterström, my wife of twenty-three years, who—wearing an unusual wool sweater she had made by hand—opened her door to a stranger on a blind date with the kindest smile I had ever seen. I would quickly discover that she was one in a million and that her love of life and dedication to making a real difference in the lives of others were simply irresistible.

Or Dr. Louis Kanda, a renowned cardiac surgeon who, in the summer of 1994, would use his considerable skill and even greater humanity to reconstruct my heart, correcting a major defect that threatened my life. It's hard to imagine that this doctor from Zaire (now the Democratic Republic of the Congo), who trained in Washington, Cleveland, and Paris, would not only come into my life but also be the only person to literally hold my heart in his hands.

Or all of the other teachers, mentors, colleagues, customers, and partners—all of whom were once strangers—who have helped me to think in new ways about the practice of business and how companies and organizations can innovate and grow by unlocking the real genius in all of their people.

Or scores of other people throughout history and today whom I've never met, who continually sparked my curiosity about people, places, ideas, inventions, and a world filled with limitless possibilities.

THE NECESSITY OF STRANGERS

In an important way, practically all of my best ideas are built on the ideas and insights of others who were at one time strangers. So you might say that I am keen on the importance, or should I say the *necessity*, of strangers and their powerful role in our lives and our success as individuals, companies, and organizations. I would even venture to guess that you might also be surprised by the powerful impact that strangers have had on your life and work. You might enjoy taking a moment or two to start your own list of important strangers as a simple way to give even greater personal meaning to the necessity of strangers in your own life. It is an idea that runs counter to the way that most of us, and most of our companies and organizations, think and act.

We live in a world filled with strangers and also in a world where most of us have been conditioned to fear or at least avoid people we don't know or understand. People whom we see as different from us in any number of ways and who can seem, by our own quick assessment, to pose a threat. Strangers we pass on the street or sit next to—sometimes uncomfortably—on the bus or the subway, or at a local restaurant or movie theater. The strangers who come to work every single day in the very same companies and organizations that we do—whom we stand next to in the elevator, pass in the hall, meet at the coffee pot or break room, or see at the holiday party. Strangers in other companies and organizations we might someday choose to work in or possibly collaborate with. Strangers who live just around the corner or halfway around the world whom we learn about in books, in magazines, online, on milk cartons, or on the radio or the nightly news. These strangers, whom we quickly choose to ignore or form an opinion about, are the people who force us out of our comfort zones and challenge us to question the knowledge, beliefs, and habits we hold dear. Most of us assume that strangers are a problem rather than a remarkable opportunity to learn, grow, and reach our full potential. It is a view that translates to our belief that the people we know best are the real keys to our success as companies, organizations, and individuals.

But what if this isn't the case? What if strangers are actually, in many ways, more important than friends? More important to our growth as individuals, more essential to the success of our companies and organizations, and more critical to the prosperity of our nations and the stability of the world we share with seven billion other strangers? And what if in order to succeed in anything worth doing we must engage, learn from, and collaborate with people we don't know, in new and compelling ways?

It may seem counterintuitive that strangers are to be embraced rather than ignored or avoided, but they are a necessity—precisely because of their differences and what they know that we don't know;

their objectivity and ability to be open and honest with us about the things that really matter; and their capacity to challenge us to think very differently about ourselves, the problems we face, and the nature of what is possible. Finding and engaging the right strangers has the power to make all of us more complete, compelling, innovative, and successful.

In fact, this premise is at the heart of my consulting work with leading companies and organizations in the United States and around the world that strive to innovate, grow, connect with customers in new and more meaningful ways, and bring out the brilliance in all their people.

It's work for which I have created the following shorthand:

Explore. Connect. Innovate. Grow.

These four simple words express not only my experience over the past twenty-five years, but also my optimistic bias that we can do more remarkable things in our work and personal lives if we are open to *exploring* the world around us, *connecting* with the right people and ideas, turning those connections and ideas into conversations and then *innovations* that matter, and using those innovations as the catalyst for business and personal *growth*.

And it is an idea that I am passionate about sharing.

WHERE STRANGERS MATTER

It turns out that in most areas critical to business and personal success, our ability to engage and learn from strangers is vital. This includes all five of the areas we'll delve into in Part Two, the first of which is *innovation* and the challenge of bringing the right new ideas to market. As we will discover in Chapter Four, real innovation and most important new ideas occur when we make connections and put together insight from strangers in other industries, places, and walks of life. As the poet Robert Frost once said: "An idea is a feat of association." It also includes the critical area of *people*. As we will see in Chapter Five, companies and organizations can reach their potential only by hiring and fully engaging the right strangers who will challenge them to reach beyond the way that things have always been done. And it includes uncovering the hidden promise of real *collaboration*. In Chapter Six we will show how bringing strangers together can unlock all of the know-how in our enterprises. We'll also show how companies and organizations can use mergers and acquisitions as a way to become more remarkable rather than simply bigger. In Chapter Seven we will see how the most astute businesses are creating powerful relationships with the strangers we call *customers* and why this is likely to be the wave of the future. In Chapter Eight, we will think about the implications for leading in a world filled with strangers. Then finally, in Chapter Nine, we will think about the importance of travel—to places near and far—and its power to break down the barriers that separate people and limit possibilities.

In each of these areas so essential to business, organizational, and personal success, strangers are a necessity, and our ability to engage the right strangers in the right ways will determine whether or not we ever reach our full potential.

I'm not simply suggesting that it is important to engage people from other cultures, countries, races, genders, or religions, although of course that is true. One of our biggest challenges as individuals and organizations is being open to and learning from people who may speak the same language as us but who think and act with very different meaning—people from other disciplines, from other walks of life, and with distinctly different personalities from ours, some of whom we might already work with. People who have different training, different expertise, and a different approach to looking at the world.

Here are a set of common challenges that underscore the real potential of strangers in our companies, organizations, and personal lives. Take a moment to look at these questions and then think about how often they come up in the place where you work and how strangers might be part of their solution.

Discovering the Value of Strangers

Business success involves answering a set of important questions. Think about the role that strangers can play in helping you find the answers to the following questions:

- Why don't we innovate more consistently and successfully?
- Why do we tend to come up with incremental improvements rather than real breakthroughs?
- Why do we have so much trouble finding, developing, engaging, and retaining the best people?
- Why do many of our most talented employees decide to leave?
- Why do we have such great difficulty collaborating in order to solve key problems and create new opportunities?
- Why is it so hard to share knowledge with each other?
- Why do our mergers and acquisitions rarely reach their business potential?
- Why is it so hard to create brand-new market opportunities and to build new customer relationships?
- Why do we have so much trouble understanding customers and their needs and aspirations?
- Why do leaders struggle to create energy and enthusiasm about growth and the future?

■ ■ ■

These questions are all about the future of business and success in a world in which all of us can—and, quite frankly, must—have access to more new ideas, insights, perspectives, and relationships than ever before. A world filled with more customers, competitors, and potential colleagues and collaborators than we ever imagined. And a world that is also filled with more personal, business, economic, and political challenges and opportunities than we can comprehend. Success in this world requires new, better, and much more open and collaborative thinking and action that includes strangers.

But if left to our own devices, we probably wouldn't turn to strangers. So let's put a bit of context around the role of friends and strangers in our success.

THE VALUE AND LIMITS OF FRIENDS

If you ask people to identify who matters most to their success, most people are likely to give you a very quick response—*friends*, of course, our closest connections in the world other than our immediate family. And for many people, friendships *are* their most important relationships—which is not surprising given the changing, more mobile nature of society and the reality that many of us no longer live in close proximity to our extended families. And that even assumes that we like and get along with most of our relatives. I'm often reminded by friends who have issues with their families that "you don't get to choose your family, but you do get to choose your friends," which suggests the outsize importance that we place on them.

And, at one level, I don't disagree. Our closest friends *are* the folks we are most likely to confide in, hang out with, party with, learn with, and grow with; the folks we feel most comfortable bouncing ideas off of; the folks we know will be there for us in good times and tough times. We ask them for guidance when we need a second opinion or to confirm our judgments when we don't feel up to facing something on our own. They've even been immortalized in one of the most popular TV shows in history, *Friends*—a show about six quirky friends going through life together in New York City. And though they weren't exactly like all of us, their less-than-settled world and less-than-settled relationships struck a sympathetic chord with viewers around the world, who enthusiastically and loyally viewed every episode for ten years (and who continue to view it in syndication).

We've also been taught to believe that friends are the real keys to our success—a teaching that can be summed up by the common notion that "it's not what you know but whom you know." Clearly, we believe as a society (and most societies around the world share this belief) that friends—especially friends in high places—are our greatest personal and professional assets. As a result, we work very hard to go to the right colleges, to live in the right neighborhoods, to work for the right companies and organizations, and to build the right circle or networks of friends. Although friends are important, their value is somewhat misunderstood and decidedly too limiting in two vital respects. First, most of us just don't have enough friends or a diverse enough set of them to give us the breadth of insight and perspectives we need to continually stretch our thinking and to grow. And second, the exact reasons why we count on friends are the same reasons that their input may not be ideal for our efforts to stretch and grow.

The Numbers Limit

To put the first concern in perspective, let's spend a moment thinking about our friends "by the numbers," and let's assume that we're all average—that is, right smack in the middle of the statistical bell curve. Now I know that very few people like to think of themselves as average, and, if you can keep a secret, I'm certainly assuming that readers of this book are way above the norm. I might even conjecture that you are similar in your profile to the residents of Lake Wobegon—the fictional Minnesota town in Garrison Keillor's popular radio show *A Prairie*

Home Companion—"where all the women are strong, all the men are good looking, and all the children are above average." But if we are average—or, using the measure of British anthropologist Robin Dunbar, if we're simply human—we are likely to have about 150 friends.[1] That's 150 other people with whom we can have a meaningful relationship based on some "personal connection and a level of trust and commitment."

Dunbar would argue that we fit a pattern along with all other primates. It's a pattern that dates back to our earliest ancestors as they hunted for game and gathered nuts and berries. These folks tended to live in villages or communities of roughly 150 people—which, according to his research, turned out to be a manageable number for living and surviving together. In earlier times it was a pretty darn significant number of people to count on and learn from. After all, there weren't that many people around, or at least not that many people we could gain access to. And there wasn't that much knowledge floating around. So if we were lucky, our group of 150 "friends" contained some very clever and very handy people. People who knew how to hunt, forage, find water, make warm clothes that wouldn't give them a rash, and make a mean guacamole, and who ideally knew how to build a perfect fire.

However, in a world that today has over seven billion people, your 150 friends constitute an incredibly small percentage of the total population.

$$150 \div 7{,}000{,}000{,}000 = 0.000000021$$

In other words, when challenged to think about and solve a pressing problem or create a new opportunity, as awesome people with an average number of friends, we're not playing with anything that approaches a full deck. And though our friends are a reasonable starting point to a broader world filled primarily with strangers, relying on friends is remarkably limiting, even if you count among your friends some of the world's leading authorities on the issues at hand.

But let's increase the number by adding in more casual acquaintances—the rest of your Facebook friends and/or your LinkedIn contacts. That should make your number quite a bit larger—maybe up to five hundred people or more—and though you don't have a lot of face time with these folks, it's reasonable to think that some might come in handy at some point in the future for reasons that seem obvious and other reasons that are less obvious but are at the heart of this book. Yet even if your "new and improved" number is five hundred or a thousand friends, it pales in significance to the number of folks that you could know, learn from, and collaborate or innovate with. The seven billion–plus just mentioned. And that doesn't include the folks who are no longer here who may have left ideas and insights to share.

So if we do the math once again, our fraction of the people we could know or connect to is dramatically higher (that is, almost seven times higher) but only slightly more impressive.

$$1,000 \div 7,000,000,000 = 0.000000142$$

That's the percentage of people on earth that one well-connected person is likely to know. So relying on our circle of friends is quite limiting. Now I can hear some of you saying that your network of 1,000 LinkedIn contacts puts you only two calls away from 13,743,301 other people, and that's certainly enough folks to have as resources in the battle for truth, justice, innovation, and greater success. And that's not a bad point at all, assuming of course that you could figure out which of these folks to reach out to—especially the ones who are very different from you—and which of your friends could begin the process by opening the first door.

The Similarity Limit

This leads us to the second limitation of our friends, because the biggest challenge isn't that we don't know very many people or that we don't know very many people that well. The biggest challenge is that the people we do know well are probably a lot like us—especially our closest friends, who are a small but very influential subset of the 150. Most of them are likely to have a very similar educational background to ours, a similar socioeconomic position, similar interests, similar views about the things that we consider important, and even a similar type of job. They may have even had a relatively similar upbringing in a relatively similar community. And, according to Bill Bishop in his book *The Big Sort*, they have probably settled into a relatively similar way of life in either our community or another community just like ours.[2] More interestingly, they are likely to see the world in a somewhat similar way and share many or most of the beliefs about living that we hold dear.

That doesn't mean that they will necessarily root for the same teams, listen to the same music, have the same hobbies, or enjoy the same foods, but in the most essential aspects of life they are a lot more like us than different from us. And, most important, they are likely to think like us, which makes them less than perfect when it comes to questioning our thinking, pushing our understanding, stirring the pot, and helping us to do new and better things. Sure, they're encouraging, but sometimes that means agreeing with us even when they shouldn't—when we'd be better served by a divergent opinion. In fact, they're typically programmed to agree with us, to see things the same way we do, and to be content with the things we are content with—whether it's because they actually do agree or because they are disinclined to undermine our plans or risk our friendship. And in our Facebook world, no one wants to be "unfriended."

All of which means that they are likely to agree with us way more often than they disagree.

Now, most of us have at least a few very eclectic friends that we are quick to point to in order to show our open-mindedness. And some of them will see the world very differently than we do and may be more likely to speak their minds when they disagree with us. But generally we tend to feel most comfortable hanging out with people who think like we do. It's simply human nature.

THE LIMITS OF BUSINESS AS USUAL

In the world of business, conformity is even more pronounced. Companies and organizations typically hire people with whom they "connect," who will fit in and get with the program, and who won't shake things up too much. Sure, we say we want to hire very different people who will bring in new ideas and perspectives, but the reality is quite the opposite. When push comes to shove, we seek out people with easily understood degrees from well-regarded colleges and universities, people with easily understood resumes and apparently successful work experiences in the things we need to get done, and people with similar backgrounds, personalities, and worldviews that will fit easily into the department and the culture we've worked hard to build.

But business and organizational success requires us to be different in ways that really matter to the customers, colleagues, and shareholders we serve. The companies and organizations that don't change are severely penalized. And even businesses that create major breakthroughs must figure out what comes next more quickly. Remember how impressed you were with Blockbuster, the video rental company? They helped to reinvent the world of home entertainment by building convenient retail stores where we could easily find all the latest movies and games. At their peak, in 2004, they had over nine thousand stores and revenues of almost $6 billion.[3] Yet somehow they got stuck in their own best thinking and couldn't reinvent their business model fast enough to meet the challenge of Netflix—a company that changed the game and made Blockbuster's stores obsolete by quickly mailing videos directly to customers. By the beginning of 2011, Netflix had over twenty-six million subscribers and seemed to be on top of the video world. But less than a year later the game was changing again and, after a few major customer relationship blunders, the smartest people at Netflix were trying to figure out how to survive in a cable TV and internet-based world dominated by digital streaming.

A world where customers had an ever-growing number of choices for content, how they received it, and how they used it.

And that's just one example of an industry turned upside down by change and an unwillingness to be open to the ideas of strangers. The same thing is happening to books, appliances, education, music, car buying, professional services, fundraising, real estate, political campaigns, and every other field in which we can drive knowledge and connect with people using technology and the power of our social networks. Social networks that are increasingly made up of strangers. This suggests that all of us, and all of the companies and organizations we work for, must continually do things in new ways just to keep up; that there is now a premium on continually being different in ways that are more valuable to customers; and that being different requires us to welcome very different people, ideas, and points of view.

What we should believe is that "it's not whom you know but whom you *could* know" that determines our success. In a small, fast-changing, and increasingly competitive world, friends and familiar colleagues simply aren't enough. Sure, we need them because they are in many ways an essential part of the equation in enabling us to do the basics well, and they are critical to our personal well-being and sense of sanity and security. But they are not going to get us all the way to where we need to go. We don't know enough, and neither do they.

The exciting news is that we now have the ability to reach out and connect with literally anyone else on the planet, including people with very different backgrounds, sets of knowledge, and perspectives on how to get important things done, and different pieces of the puzzles we are trying to solve—or totally different puzzles that could change our world. It is a prospect that wasn't nearly as easy even ten years ago. But now, when faced with a challenge or an opportunity that matters, we don't need to think about only what we know or whom we know. Instead, we can imagine what we would *like* to know and find the people who know it. That is a remarkably liberating proposition and a great equalizer for businesses and organizations of all sizes, because in today's world of networks and potential connections, the companies, organizations, and individuals that make exploration and openness part of their DNA have a better chance to win.

And that's where the real power of strangers can change the equation.

So now imagine this new paradigm:

Business and Personal Success =
What I Already Know +
My Knowledge or Understanding Gap +
A Stranger (or Strangers) Who Knows How to Fill It

But first, we have to overcome our aversion to people we don't know, armed with a strong belief that they really do matter. And that means understanding more clearly why we tend to avoid, dismiss, and even fear strangers. Then we have to figure out how to create a new habit of openness, engagement, and embracing possibilities.

TWO

Aversion

Civilization is the encouragement of differences.
—MAHATMA GANDHI

L et's go back to my walk to the bus stop with our daughter Carly and a moment in time when my aversion to strangers, disguised as fatherly instinct, got the better of me. After all, most of us have been conditioned to believe that strangers are dangerous—through books, movies, the media, the cautionary guidance of family and friends, and even our own *humanity*. Maybe we're simply wired to fear or avoid strangers through some combination of nurture and nature. We even have a phrase, "stranger danger," that is part of our collective vocabulary and highlights the reality that there *are* some very bad people out there—strangers who pose a real threat to our children, break into our homes, steal our identities, try to con us online or over the phone, pollute our communities and natural places, bring drugs into our neighborhoods, and create unthinkable horrors like 9/11. Strangers to be avoided. People whose scary faces are found on post office walls, in nightly news reports, and in the looks of everyone else we see who bears any resemblance to their images. Like the fellow on our walk to the bus. A fellow who might have been perfectly harmless and just different.

It's not only a fear for our own safety and well-being that keeps most of us from connecting with and learning from strangers. Most of us also have an aversion to people whose ideas, knowledge, insights, backgrounds, perspectives, questions, beliefs, approaches, customs, and behaviors are different from ours. An aversion that is also wired into our brains. And we'll need to understand why, in order to unlock the real value and necessity of strangers in our work and lives. So let me begin with a few stories about our perceptions about other people to set the stage. Then we'll look briefly at the insight of leading business thinkers, psychologists, and neuroscientists.

As a child I had a keen interest in geography, places, and people and would spend countless hours sitting on the plush olive green carpet on our living room floor (totally trendy at the time) studying maps, reading the latest issues of *National Geographic*, collecting stamps, and imagining what life was like in every corner of the globe. These were definitely not the "coolest" of kids' activities for someone growing up in Northern California, not even for someone who also played a lot of basketball and baseball and skateboarded down some semi-insane hills. But I now realize these interests helped to shape my sense of the world and all of its amazing possibilities.

Armed with my trusty red Hammond *New World Atlas and Gazetteer*, I would trace the paths of mighty rivers, hop between the tallest mountains, take ships across vast oceans to wondrous ports of call, and make daily journeys to all of the world's capitals. Once there, I would imagine wandering through grand bazaars; entering majestic temples; attending great festivals; and meeting with kings, queens, tribal chiefs, government officials, and children who would eagerly instruct me in the exotic and everyday secrets of their countries and cultures. Then, for my part, I would always offer them cold milk and warm cookies in an attempt to be a thoughtful and appreciative guest. I'm not exactly sure how I expected the milk to remain cold and the cookies to stay warm, but such is the power of imagination.

Then, for added insight, I would turn to the pages of my stamp album and study the small squares and rectangles that told even more tales of every country's history, geography, people, politics, leaders, generals, natural wonders, animals, and ideas that made each place unique and, in its own way, special. Stamps that helped me to better understand a world that was, at that time, shared by three billion people. Or, more precisely, three billion strangers—not including my very limited circle of relatives, friends, classmates, and neighbors.

Three billion people whom I didn't know yet, living in distant lands that I longed to visit. And at the age of nine I imagined a life filled with travel, exploration, and learning. A life of meeting new people and discovering as many corners of the globe as possible. In the process, I would also discover the things that made us all the same, and the things that made us different. Though at the time I'm not sure I really understood the simple notion that our similarities provide the basis for connecting as humans even as our differences provide a richness of possibilities that can, with an open mind, make us all more complete. Though certainly I had no reason to think otherwise. I felt no aversion to all of these strangers.

I also remember having a keen fascination with places where no one lived, especially the cold, mysterious, and desolate continent of Antarctica hanging out at the bottom of every world map. A place viewed by many as the final frontier, a land—if you could call its icy terrain "land"—where no civilization had ever formed. The only completely uninhabited place on earth, and, thanks to a remarkable quirk of history, a perfect place to understand our aversion to strangers and its real cost.

THE RACE TO THE SOUTH POLE

By the end of the nineteenth century, humans had traveled across most of the earth's surface. They had explored and settled six of its seven continents, journeyed the length of the world's great rivers and endless oceans, visited most of its islands—including some very remote dots in the Pacific—trekked across its largest deserts, hiked through its densest jungles and rainforests, and climbed to the top of all but its highest and most treacherous mountains. And during this long period of exploration and settlement, humans created roughly seven thousand distinct cultures,[1] each of which had their own stories, languages, beliefs, and knowledge base, and unique and powerful insights that often never made it beyond their known worlds.

Sure, people missed a few things, especially in terms of understanding the worlds that existed beneath the earth's seas, but given the tools and technologies they had at their disposal, humans were pretty clever explorers, pretty skilled settlers and adapters, and pretty impressive discoverers of the wonders and mysteries of the planet. And as the year 1900 approached, there were only a few more "unreachable" places to check off. A kind of bucket list, you might say, for those with a burning desire to reach uncharted territory. Among these, the biggest prize that captivated the imagination was Antarctica, specifically the South Pole—the southernmost point on earth, in a land so harsh that few could even envision getting there, let alone spending time there.

But sparked by the power of curiosity, the promise of fame or great personal achievement, and a lecture by Professor John Murray to the Royal Geographic Society in 1893 advocating for research on Antarctica to "resolve the outstanding geographical questions still posed in the south," the race to explore the seventh continent and reach the magnetic bottom of the earth was on.[2]

From 1897 to 1912 fourteen expeditions from eight nations— Belgium, the United Kingdom, Germany, Sweden, France, Japan, Norway, and Australia—all set sail for Antarctica for "scientific and other purposes." Each expedition improved our understanding of Antarctica's geography, terrain, and climate, and the natural life that somehow survived there. And each got closer to the ultimate prize of reaching the South Pole or what chronicler Roland Huntsford called "the last place on earth" in his book of the same title.[3]

At the center of this final effort in 1910 were Robert Falcon Scott, a British naval officer and explorer who had led an earlier Antarctic expedition between 1901 and 1904, and Roald Amundsen, a Norwegian explorer who had been the first person to traverse the Northwest Passage on the other side of the globe. By 1910, as each set out on a quest to reach the South Pole first, they were likely viewed as two of the most remarkable explorers of their era, but they were two men with distinctly different objectives, interests, and worldviews. And two men with distinctly different views of the importance of strangers.

Scott was a product of Victorian and Edwardian England who devoted his career to the Navy and to the goal of personal advancement. Some experts have suggested that he really wasn't that interested in being an explorer but viewed exploration as a path to acclaim in a society that valued bravery and honor. And, by most accounts, he did not particularly believe that planning, preparation, or having direct and relevant experience were keys to success. In fact, he seemed to have an aversion to them. For Scott, the key was setting a bold and widely known objective; he could always improvise along the way in order to achieve it.

Amundsen, on the other hand, was the son of a Norwegian ship owner and sea captain and was deeply committed to a life of exploration. Viewed by many as a true genius, he could not have been more different from Scott in his approach. Amundsen relied on an uncommon commitment to planning, preparation, practicality, and learning from others. In his mind, nothing that could be understood in advance should be left to chance. He also kept everything to himself, not even telling the members of his own party that they were heading to the South Pole until they were halfway there.

Triumph and Tragedy

But let's fast-forward to the end of the story (spoiler alert!), then give you a bit of explanation for why things turned out the way they did. Amundsen's team would reach the South Pole first on December 14,

1911, then return home safely, earning the world's praise but fewer headlines than one might have guessed. Scott's team would reach the South Pole on January 17, 1912, thirty-four days later, then die of cold and starvation on the trek back across Antarctica. They would receive both the world's sympathy for paying the ultimate price in such a heroic quest and an amazing amount of publicity and notoriety for years to follow. Modest reward for someone with a relentless aversion to learning from people who were very different from him.

Amundsen realized at the beginning of his quest that any effort to reach the South Pole would require a deep understanding of how to survive in the harshest of environments. As a result, he studied and analyzed every bit of available information he could find on living in, traversing, and ultimately surviving in brutal cold. But he would also need more practical knowledge of what to wear, how to shelter, how to be outside in severe temperatures, how to move on snow and ice, what to eat and how to arrange it, how to avoid scurvy—a known cause of danger—and all of the other things that could go wrong along the way. And he would need to make the right decisions about the animals that he should bring—essential partners in any polar journey—and the most appropriate size and skills for an expeditionary team that could work together to accomplish the objective and survive. His research served him well, but Amundsen would rely most heavily on his own firsthand knowledge of Antarctica and similar environments gained from two earlier journeys. He had served as first mate on the *Belgica* as part of the Belgian Antarctic Expedition from 1897 to 1899. This expedition, captained by Adrien de Gerlache, was the first to stay over the winter in the Antarctic Circle, a fate determined when the ship became icebound.

Amundsen had also captained his own ship, the *Gjøa*, through the Northwest Passage from 1903 to 1906. On this second journey north he spent two years living among the Inuits and studying their lives in great detail. He was intrigued by how these native people used and cared for their dogs, their clothing and diet, and everything they did each time they left the relative warmth of their dwellings and headed out on the snow. This openness to learning from strangers would inform all of his planning and prove to be vital to Amundsen's eventual success.

Scott, on the other hand, was not inclined to learn from the experience of others, especially "primitive" people who lived in climates comparable to that of the South Pole—even if they understood how to adapt. For him, and for his peers in England, experts in the established scientific community were the only sources of knowledge to be trusted. Unfortunately, no one in any of the British institutions of science and higher education had particular expertise regarding the elements of this endeavor. In fact, it could be argued that Scott himself was the leading British expert on polar exploration by virtue of having made an earlier expedition to Antarctica from 1901 to 1904. Though it had been a trip fraught with problems, including scurvy, it apparently never dawned on Scott that the best way to survive and navigate these terrains might be to learn from people who had lived there for generations. Learning from "locals," as it were, was not part of the method of leading scientists at home. Although they spent considerable time studying the world's people and cultures— and, some might suggest, exploiting them—the thought that they would view native peoples as equals, or in this case as even superior, wasn't even a consideration. Ruled by this aversion to strangers, Scott would make a series of inadequate arrangements and calculations.

First, Scott's team would begin sixty miles (or ninety-six kilometers) farther from the Pole—a difference in distance that mattered considerably in such a harsh climate. Second, Scott's plan relied on a combination of ponies, mechanical sledges, dogs, and the human hauling of provisions. He based this decision on the prevailing view of experts in England that dogs were of limited value in transport. Amundsen knew better, and early on it became clear to Scott and his team that neither the horses nor the sledges, which developed technical problems near the start, were suited to the Antarctic environment. Scott also lacked sufficient knowledge about the use and care of the dogs. And he and his team weren't particularly good skiers, which meant they could not keep up with the dogs unless they weighed the dogs down and sapped their strength.

Amundsen and his men, on the other hand, were expert skiers who understood that it was easier to ski than to walk on snow. Not a big surprise, given that they were Norwegians and likely began skiing at a young age. They also understood the importance of resting their animals and themselves for considerable periods of time, and the importance of eating lots of protein and taking vitamin C in order to maintain strength and prevent scurvy. Keeping the animals strong was essential because, unlike Scott, they knew that they should rely on the dogs to haul provisions.

The Critical Difference

When I first read the story of the race to the South Pole many years ago, I was struck by the notion that curiosity, openness, and the practical knowledge both of and acquired from strangers were the real keys to success. Amundsen understood that there were people—albeit very different from him in many ways—who knew essential parts of the equation for living and traveling in a polar climate, and he was eager to gain their insight in order to achieve his goal. This mindset, combined with careful planning, made the difference. Scott, on the other hand, believed that he had, by virtue of his upbringing and training, the right knowledge to succeed. For things he didn't know, he would turn to the guidance of people like himself, and if *they* didn't know the answers, he assumed that the answers didn't exist. His aversion to learning from "strangers" proved to be his downfall.

If we can take one very positive lesson away from Scott, it is the notion that sometimes we need to improvise as we go along. But this improvisation should be based on being as prepared as possible.

It is instructive to think about this moment one hundred years ago and how it relates to our lives today and the lives of our companies and organizations. In one sense we are all like Scott—strongly committed to the adequacy of our own knowledge and expertise and averse to learning from others, especially others who are very different from us. We can attribute much of his view to the time and place he came from, with its powerful belief in the power of its science and the superiority of its own culture, but to what do we attribute our own insistence on the power of our expertise and the limited value of strangers? It strikes me that we don't have such a handy excuse. In a world where it is estimated that knowledge is now doubling every twelve months[4], we should be way more humble and way more open to the ideas and insights of others. And we should be keen to reinvent our definition of expertise to include greater openness to finding the right knowledge no matter where it comes from.

Which leads us back to Amundsen and his simple, or some might say difficult, formula for success—a formula summarized as follows:

This formula is simple because it is, at least on paper, not very different from the process that most of us and most companies

---

Creating a Process for Success

- Determine your objective and the compelling result you hope to achieve.
- Develop an initial plan to achieve it.
- Determine the knowledge and know-how required and the gaps in your understanding and abilities.
- Find strangers with the knowledge to fill those gaps—people for whom that knowledge is second nature.
- Invest the time and effort to learn from them in order to fill your gaps.
- Revise your plan based on your new learning.
- Execute the plan with some flexibility, being open to making necessary adjustments along the way.

---

and organizations try to follow in doing anything important. And it is difficult because we are challenged to be honest about our gaps and then equally challenged in our willingness to stretch our thinking about where we might turn for help. This is where our aversion to strangers comes into play. Like Scott, we tend to turn to the usual suspects—friends, colleagues, and experts in our field or industry whose insights are understandable and align with our thinking—and clearly *not* people from other places, disciplines, or walks of life, who we are sure could never really understand the unique nature of our businesses.

I remember many consulting projects in which I suggested that customers look for insight in some less-than-usual places, like science and modern art museums, music performances, preschools, nature, bustling neighborhoods, other industries that seemed worlds away, and even other cultures—only to be told that such different ideas from such different people and places would never work. These were places whose ideas had never been tried in their worlds of information technology, government contracting, pharmaceutical manufacturing, health care and wellness, hospitality, new car sales, or financial services. These ideas stirred a real aversion on the part of people who were vested in a certain way of doing things. Yet, in large part, these "new" ideas and sources of inspiration for innovation, engagement, efficiency, and delivering greater value ultimately drove greater success because they were different. And in the case of Amundsen, they reinforced his formula.

Amundsen's experience also suggests an intriguing question. What if, instead of actively avoiding the ideas of people we don't understand, as Scott did, we were to live with complete strangers? Not for years, but long enough to begin to understand how they live, the things they value, and the knowledge and wisdom they have accumulated through generations of engaging the world and each other. And what if we were open rather than averse to the possibility that some of these things might significantly improve our chances of achieving the objectives we hold dear? Obviously we would need to pick the right strangers with ties to what we hope to accomplish and then ask them the right questions— though there is a case to be made for choosing *any* strangers and for opening ourselves to the reality that there are multiple worldviews that are worthy of being heard. As smart as we are, or our companies and organizations are, we can never know everything there is to know about the things that concern us most. Our real aversion should be to seeing our own thinking as the only way to move forward.

THE REAL CHALLENGE OF PEOPLE WHO ARE DIFFERENT

Let me give you a business example that highlights the surprising cost of our aversion to the most common of strangers—those who pass by us each and every day.

In 2008, after investing more than $600 million, the U.S. Census Bureau decided to scrap its plan for equipping census takers with handheld computers. As a result, the 2010 census was conducted much like the first U.S. census back in 1790, when people went door-to-door with pencil and paper, or quill and paper, asking questions of citizens and dutifully recording their answers by hand. I guess it is reassuring to know that some things never change. But in an era in which awesome and even straightforward innovations in information technology have revolutionized business and enabled greater efficiencies and cost savings, one is left to wonder why the Census Bureau dropped the ball. And given that this screw-up resulted in an additional $3 billion cost to the taxpayers, one is even more amazed to realize that this screw-up didn't need to happen.[5]

Missing the Obvious

Shortly after the decision to cancel the handheld computer initiative was announced, I had the opportunity to give a speech to an association of government CIOs on innovation and learning from strangers. When the topic of the census was raised by someone in the audience, I suggested that this mistake would have been avoidable had the powers that be been open to a world of strangers and powerful ideas, and that they should have never committed to creating a "custom" solution when their problem had already been solved. In fact, I suggested that the answer to their problem was right under their noses and that it literally visited them every single workday. I then wondered aloud whether they had ever paid attention to a group of men and women wearing very stylish brown uniforms and driving equally stylish brown trucks, who dropped off and picked up packages at their offices. Folks who carried handheld computers to record and track their work—handheld computers that one can only assume contained every address in America. Folks who might have been willing to share what they knew about handheld computers and collecting data at millions of addresses because it was probably in their interest to be kind to the federal government.

"Really?" someone countered. "Do you really believe that business can be that simple?"

"In many cases I actually do," I replied without hesitation. "I believe that we have the ability to find brilliance in the world around us when we keep our eyes open and are willing to engage strangers. The real challenge is to find the right strangers, though in this case it strikes me that they were waiting to be discovered."

Getting Beyond Business as Usual

I realize that government agencies and corporate departments work hard to receive the largest budget possible as a way to achieve their missions. I also realize that they rarely decide to ask for less money, or less staff, or less of anything unless they are under great pressure to cut back. The size of one's budget is viewed by many as a clear sign of worth and, as a result, drives many decisions about the right initiatives and the very nature of innovation. But should this keep us from being open to strangers?

There must be a reason, or a set of reasons, why some of us don't seem to notice the UPS guy or gal—reasons that go beyond simply trying to maintain our budget. Could it be that we have an aversion to learning from people in brown work uniforms, driving trucks and delivering packages? That the work they do and the business they are in don't fit with the idea of the very important work we are trying to accomplish? Or that we regard them as irrelevant to solving our problem—a problem that requires our own original thinking and a much higher degree of expertise and sophistication? Or that we have already chosen a path and find it impossible to accept any additional input that could call our work into question? Or perhaps it is something else entirely.

But before we can overcome our aversion, we have to understand more about why we behave the way we do. To do this, let's take a quick look at what science has to say.

WHAT SCIENCE TELLS US

The fields of psychology and neuroscience provide valuable insight into our aversion to strangers. It is fascinating stuff, because it leads us to realize that some combination of our wiring and upbringing makes most of us think like Scott did a hundred years ago and like the folks at the Census Bureau did more recently. There is a lot more detail than I can get into here, but I'd like to share some of the most interesting and relevant thinking as part of the context for changing the way we look at and engage people who are different from us. To make this change, we need to think about the nature of our prejudices and inclination to stereotype others; the challenge of groupthinking and our tendency to conform; our attachment, from an early age, to only a few people; our belief that we are right even when we aren't; and the notion of "inattentional blindness" to things and people who cross our paths. All are pieces of the aversion puzzle.

Stereotyping and Prejudice

In their 2013 article "The Nature of Implicit Prejudice: Implications for Personal and Public Policy," psychologists Mahzarin Banaji of Harvard and Curtis Hardin of Brooklyn College suggest, based on a detailed review of the latest research across disciplines, that traditional thinking about stereotyping and prejudice based on ignorance, animosity, and hatred explains only part of the world today.[6] They contend that the real challenge is implicit prejudice: "In short, we now know that the operation of prejudice and stereotyping in social judgment and behavior does not require personal animus, hostility or even awareness. In fact, prejudice is often 'implicit'—that is, unwitting, unintentional, and uncontrollable—even among the most well-intentioned people." They cite a wide range of studies, many of which they have been part of, that look at ethnicity and race, gender, sexual orientation, body shape, age, and adolescents. And they surmise that these prejudices "develop early in children across cultures and appear to involve specific brain structures associated with non-rational thought." They support this understanding by arguing that even with clear public policies to address discrimination, prejudice remains firmly part of the cultural landscape.

Stereotyping and prejudice are an even greater concern if we have an implicit tendency to pass judgment on people who are different from us in some way—if we are wired to marginalize them. It could be that this tendency is part of the reason why we have so much trouble engaging and learning from strangers.

All of us have also been conditioned to think about other people in terms of the stereotypes—both good and bad—that we hold. So our minds quickly go to a set of preconceived notions. And these stereotypes tend to come out in conversations and jokes at parties, picnics, bars, and other social events, and even at the office, when any of us, no matter what our background is (and surrounded by other people like us), think it's okay to be funny at someone else's expense.

Which is probably why I find the following joke, or rather anti-joke, and others like it to be so helpful in challenging our thinking about people, innovation, collaboration, leadership, learning, creating great customer experiences, and the real keys to business and personal success.

"Why do Christians believe in God?"

Brief pause while you come up with an answer . . .

"Because believing in God is fundamental to their belief system. If they didn't believe in God, they simply wouldn't be Christians. Muslims, Jews, and people following any other religion that believes in a god are in the same predicament."

The answer is probably not what you or I expected. We often find humor in other people's religion, rather than appreciating the greater similarities in what most of us believe.

As a result, all too often we are quick to pass judgment about other people based on the color of their skin, their ethnic or cultural backgrounds, beliefs, politics, personality types, jobs or roles, expertise and training, or a host of other things that make them "different" from us. We believe that these differences make them unlikely to be the perfect colleagues, collaborators, bosses, business partners, or potential customers. If they happen to be strangers, we are even more likely to place greater emphasis on these stereotypes as deal-breakers that keep us from engaging them and gaining their perspectives and insights. So whether our prejudice is implicit or explicit, it is a challenge to reaching our full potential.

We all do it to different degrees, harboring notions about homeless people asking for money at a traffic light, or "rednecks" selling firewood out of the back of an old pickup truck, or geeks or nerds, or stay-at-home moms, or teenagers wearing hoodies, or street performers, or New Yorkers, or recent immigrants, or old people having difficulty crossing the street, or the unemployed, or Wall Street bankers, or people in other countries, or women with their heads covered, or people with disabilities, or anyone who looks like they could pose a threat, or people who are just too different. And even when someone shows us the value of a different reality—like Katherine Boo in her powerful book *Behind the Beautiful Forevers*,[7] which challenges us to appreciate the great dignity, resourcefulness, and potential to be found in even the poorest corners of Mumbai; or Isabel Fonseca in *Bury Me Standing*,[8] a passionate story of the rich culture and history of the Roma or gypsies, one of the least under-stood and least valued people on earth; or anthropologist Wade Davis, whose studies of cultures provide a dynamic and energizing picture of the power of differences in enriching all of us[9]—we still struggle to get past our preconceived notions.

What makes this even more frustrating is the fact that all of us are, at least in terms of our genetic makeup, 99.9 percent the same by virtue of being human.[10] Granted, there is a lot of diversity in our 0.1 percent difference that tends to provoke our aversion to strangers. But our real challenge or opportunity comes when we choose to focus on the differences that matter—the ones that could be combined with what we already know to make us more complete and more successful.

Conformity and Groupthinking

In a 1952 article in *Fortune* magazine that preceded his classic book *The Organization Man*, William H. Whyte coined the term "group-think" to describe the tendency of people in companies and organi-zations to conform—that is, to follow the leader or go along with the group even when they know that there could be a better way or that the decision being made is wrong.[11] He wrote: "We are not talking about mere instinctive conformity—it is, after all, a perennial failing of mankind. What we are talking about is a rationalized conformity—an open, articulate philosophy which holds that group values are not only expedient but right and good as well." And more than sixty years later these words still ring true in most companies and organizations.

Psychologist Irving Janis built on Whyte's thinking by suggesting that "the more amiability and esprit de corps there is among the members of a policy-making in-group, the greater the danger that independent critical thinking will be replaced by groupthink." His research identified eight symptoms of groupthinking—"invulnerability," "rationale," "morality," "stereotypes," "pressure," "self-censorship," "unanimity," and "mindguards"—that act to limit a group's ability to consider and evaluate alternatives or its openness to doing so, when it comes to making important decisions.[12]

Clearly, groupthinking is great for building harmony and consensus, but not so great for stretching our thinking and being open to different ideas and ways of doing things. And it's not surprising that most organizations today continue to reward conformity and incremental thinking. Why shake things up in pursuit of an unproven way of doing things when we seem to be doing fine? Besides, aren't you "on board" and a "team player"? Don't you "buy into" our mission and the goals we're trying to accomplish? Aren't we "aligned"? These are new terms to describe an age-old phenomenon: as much as we claim to want divergent opinions and fresh thinking, most of our companies and organizations do not reward people who question authority or the status quo—even when they have reason to. In the world of groupthinking, the questions and insights of strangers can be dangerous for the organization and a career-limiting move for the person trying to broaden our frame of reference. Groupthink causes companies and organizations to have an aversion to people and ideas that are different from their accepted ways of doing things and that might call into question how they engage the world around them and how they define and address its limits and possibilities.

Besides, doesn't new thinking or additional input complicate the task of running a business and making a profit? Isn't it much easier to just move forward and get the job done? Isn't it much wiser to stay on task, limit input, and not get consumed by a bigger and more complicated world of challenges and possibilities?

For the answers, consider the Deepwater Horizon disaster that occurred in the Gulf of Mexico in 2010. According to testimony after the fact, employees at British Petroleum (BP) and partners Trans-ocean and Halliburton expressed safety concerns and even made recommendations for changes that might have prevented the oil rig from exploding.[13] Some employees even suggested that they could have stopped operations without getting the approval of senior management. Instead, groupthink prevailed, and everyone along the chain of command decided to ignore clear warnings and to agree that everything was okay.

When groupthink is prevalent, it is hard to be open even to people we know and presumably trust when they have a different opinion or a change of heart about the best course of action. After all, we've made an investment in the path we are taking, and there is safety in agreement and safety in numbers. And what are the odds that an outlier will be right? Certainly not great enough to suggest the need for a change in direction.

So even though most individuals, companies, and organizations claim that they want to be more innovative, "outside the box," and open to new ideas and possibilities, there is a powerful tendency to conform, keep plodding along in the same direction, and value people who agree with us—people who conform to, and confirm, our prevailing approach and wisdom.

How many of you remember Solomon Asch's classic experiment from the 1950s to test individual conformity to the decisions of the majority—even when the majority is obviously wrong?[14] In this experiment, participants are shown one card with a line on it and then another card with three lines of different lengths (see Figure 2.1).

Participants are then asked to pick the line on the second card that is the same length as the line on the original card. It seems simple enough, but a group of "confederates" are enlisted to stir the pot. When

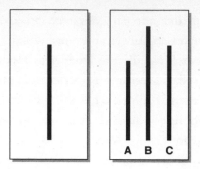

Figure 2.1 Asch's Experiment with Conformity

these confederates choose the correct answer, in this case line C, more that 99 percent of participants quickly give the correct answer as well. But when the confederates as a group choose the wrong answer, participants pick the wrong answer 32 percent of the time. The results, documented in a number of YouTube videos with a range of different groups, are quite amusing and show the power of conformity in getting us to question our own ideas and thought processes—even when they are correct. Many of us would rather get along and be wrong than be right by being different. It is a frustrating reality that also affects our openness—or lack thereof—to new people and divergent ideas.

Attachment Theory

There is also interesting and relevant research suggesting that we are wired to avoid strangers at a very early age. In studies beginning in the 1940s, John Bowlby, a British psychologist and psychiatrist, showed that infants form a powerful attachment to their mothers, or another established substitute, which provides an anchor in the world and a "secure base" from which to explore and grow.[15] This relationship not only protects them from strangers and perceived stress or danger but also acts to limit their comfort and inclination for social interactions with people they do not know well. They don't even need to be told about "stranger danger"—it's already baked in.

It is interesting to ponder how attachment theory might translate to adults in companies and organizations. There seems to be a tendency for us to build strong attachments to our bosses and members of our specific teams—seeking the safety and protection of the group and its way of working, solving problems, and creating new opportunities, rather than reaching out to strangers and new groups of people with different ideas, perspectives, and approaches—similar to the attachment children form with their mothers.

Believing We Know Best

In his book *On Being Certain*, neurologist Robert Burton suggests another possibility—that we are often convinced we are right about things even when we aren't.[16] If this is the case, it is easy to see why we would be averse to learning from others, especially others who have very different thoughts about the issues and opportunities we face. Burton argues that instead of being open to other ideas that could stretch or improve our understanding, we often have a tendency to rally around the things we believe are true even when we are presented with evidence to the contrary. He also contends that we can't really control it because our determined sense of certainty "arises out of involuntary brain mechanisms that, like love or anger, function independently of reason."[17]

If you take an honest look at your company or organization, you are likely to see this idea in action. Are there things that go on in your workplace that just don't make sense? Are there business practices, processes, and procedures that simply fly in the face of logic but that people believe are absolutely the right things to do? And when problems arise, is there a tendency to circle the wagons and do more of the same? It could be a case of groupthink or pressure to conform. But it could also be the prevailing sense that we know exactly what we're doing even when we might not have a clue, that we are simply hanging on because we don't have the insight, capability, or willingness to change.

Invisible Gorillas

Now let's add one more big idea to the mix—the possibility that we often don't notice strangers and their ideas and insights even when they cross directly in front of us. This notion, also known as "inattentional blindness," has been examined in the book *The Invisible Gorilla* by Christopher Chambris and Daniel Simons. In their well-known experiment, a group of subjects are asked to watch a video in which two groups of people dressed in white and black T-shirts are playing a game of catch with a basketball. The subjects are told to count the number of passes made by one of the two teams. Seems straightforward enough, though it requires a measure of concentration. But partway through the game a woman walks through the scene wearing a gorilla suit, and roughly 50 percent of the subjects never see her. We are left to think about the extent to which we all have blinders on and are so task-driven that we are unable to look up and see something unique or remarkable in our midst.[18] This explains why the folks at the Census Bureau were so determined to do things their own way that they were unable to notice the folks from UPS and their handheld devices—even though the bureau had a compelling need for an effective handheld computer.

There are a number of possible reasons why we are averse to strangers; it's not simply the fact that we live in fear of them or have some innate or well-developed prejudice that limits our ability to value them and connect in meaningful ways. We are actually wired to go along with, and attach ourselves to, our own groups—whether they are defined as our companies, departments, areas of knowledge and expertise, or closest friends and coconspirators. And we also are inclined to believe that we are right and to focus on the task at hand.

That doesn't mean that we can't change our habits or go against our nature. If it did, we would have to simply resign ourselves to never reaching our full potential. Besides, lots of people and organizations seem to have cracked the code in their ability to be more open to strangers and other ways of doing things. But it does suggest that we are up against a bit of a challenge in understanding and leveraging an essential missing piece for our greater success as individuals, companies, and organizations. It also suggests that we need to work to create a more open and less averse mindset.

THREE

Mindset

Where there is an open mind there will always be a frontier.
—CHARLES KETTERING

Roughly five hundred years ago the Spanish explorer and conquistador Juan Ponce de Leon—I'm not exactly sure which of these two titles was on his business card—began his quest for the "Fountain of Youth." A member of Columbus's second voyage to the New World in 1493, he remained in the western hemisphere and became not only the first European to set foot in Florida but the first Spanish governor of what is now part of the Dominican Republic. But his real passion was his determination to find a legendary spring that would provide eternal life and health simply from drinking its waters. It was an interesting idea that was captivating to some people in his era and remains a source of wonder and mystery to many people today who have to settle for Botox, plastic surgery, and some rather distasteful protein smoothies in their efforts to ward off the effects of aging.

But the coolest thing about Ponce de Leon was his mindset and his curiosity and openness to the idea that somewhere people had figured out how to live forever.

Although Ponce de Leon didn't end up finding the Fountain of Youth, he did establish St. Augustine, Florida—a relatively nice place in its own right, but not someplace that has cracked the code on how to live forever. Still, Americans today live relatively long lives when compared to people in the 1500s (and many of the world's current inhabitants), and we might ascribe this good fortune to our general understanding of health, along with key medical advances that have allowed us to eliminate or at least control certain diseases and counteract certain bad behaviors related to our diet and level of exercise.

U.S. residents now live roughly 78.5 years on average. Pretty good for a place where a significant percentage of citizens have limited access to quality health care and an even greater percentage are at least somewhat larger and more out of shape than they should be. But we don't come close to ranking in the top ten in terms of longevity, and we are more than eleven years behind the leader—which happens to be the small nation of Monaco, where the average lifespan is 89.5 years. Okay, maybe it's not a fair comparison. After all, aren't most people in Monaco rich, and don't they all have access to free health care? Probably so, though experts are more inclined to credit their long lives to the combination of a Mediterranean diet and their relaxing and relatively stress-free lifestyle as well as their clean physical environment.

Japan comes in second, with an average life expectancy of just under 84.5 years—often attributed to their diet, which emphasizes fish, vegetables, fruit, smaller portions, and eating more mindfully.

So if I wanted to figure out how to live a long and healthy life, I might keep searching for an eternal spring, I might try to crack the genetic code, I might hope for some medical miracle, or I might simply decide to go to a place where they live the longest and figure out how to mirror their lifestyle, realizing—of course—that I started this competition with my own unique genetic profile. Which of these paths I choose will depend on my mindset: how open I am to a range of new ideas and possibilities, including ideas and possibilities that come from strangers and are very different from what I already believe.

And if I really wanted to figure out how to live the longest and healthiest life possible, I might ask if I could spend time with the Melis family of the village of Perdasdefogu in the mountains of Sardinia. The nine children of this family are now a combined 818 years old, which translates to an average age of 91. Consolata is the oldest, at 105, and Mafalda is the youngest, at 78. And between them are Claudina (99), Maria (97), Antonino (93), Concetta (91), Adolfo (89), Vitalio (86), and Vitalia (80).[1] I might also want to try to be a Sardinian woman, as they seem to really live the longest. But it's not just the Melis family. Sardinia has one of the highest percentages of centenarians in the world.

Like the residents of Monaco, the Melis family has thrived on eating a simple Mediterranean diet that includes plenty of fresh fruits and vegetables, especially pears and prunes; local sheep and goat cheeses; minestrone soup; and red wine. They also attribute their good health to "physical activity, hard work, and being surrounded by loved ones." Of course, genetics, the level of stress in our lives, and the environment matter too. But the basic picture is relatively simple and clear to follow if I have the appropriate mindset to be open to it.

Or I could decide to live my life with a more typical American set of habits—which include plenty of fast food, saturated fats, refined sugars, sodium, calories, preservatives, packaged convenience foods, large portions, limited exercise, loved ones who no longer live close by, and a heaping tablespoon of stress—in the hope that either medicine or good old-fashioned luck will bring me the greatest possible longevity.[2] Or I could set out in search of another way.

Our mindset is how we are wired *or* choose to engage the world around us; it determines or predetermines the likelihood that we will reach our full potential. We have a choice: we can approach any challenge or opportunity we face with a belief that we, and the people we know best, have the requisite knowledge and skills to address it.

Or we can approach any challenge and opportunity we face with a belief that we don't have all the answers and, although we may be able to figure out the right solution, there may be other folks we don't currently know who hold the secret to a more effective or remarkable result. And we can approach any challenge or opportunity with a belief that there are limits to what is possible for ourselves and our organizations, or with a belief that the only limits are our imagination and the collective wisdom of a world filled with strangers and possibilities. We might not find the mythical Fountain of Youth that Ponce de Leon envisioned, but certainly we can hope for the prospect of a century of good health. It depends largely on our mindset and the related habits we choose to develop. I want you to think about having the right mindset to reach your full potential as a company, an organization, and an individual.

THE IMPORTANCE OF MINDSET

In *Mindset: The New Psychology of Success*, psychologist Carol Dweck suggests that people live according to one of two distinct mindsets. She calls these "fixed" and "growth" mindsets.[3]

In a fixed mindset, people believe that "their traits are just givens. They have a certain amount of brains and talent and nothing can change that. If they have a lot, they're all set, but if they don't . . . So people in this mindset worry about their traits and how adequate they are. They have something to prove to themselves and others."[4]

In a growth mindset, people "see their qualities as things that can be developed through their dedication and effort. Sure they're happy if they're brainy or talented, but that's just the starting point. They understand that no one has ever accomplished great things—not Mozart, Darwin, or Michael Jordan—without years of passionate practice and learning."[5] Dweck then goes on to suggest that people who engage the world with a fixed mindset are less open to new ways of thinking or new ways of doing things. They are more focused on the results they are able to achieve with the innate abilities they have, less open to feedback from others unless it happens to be positive and confirms their knowledge and worth, and disinclined to learn for the sake of learning unless it is tied directly to getting a better result on the task at hand—like taking a test or gaining a coveted promotion. They also seem to be far less resilient when things don't go well.

In contrast, people with a growth mindset are more curious, willing to try new things, open to constructive feedback that helps them to continue to develop their level of understanding and skills, and eager to learn for the sake of learning and personal growth. They are also much more resilient in the face of setbacks, using them as even greater inspiration for growth. For them, life and work are a journey to greater mastery, and even the subject or subjects of that mastery can change and develop over time as they see the value of new learning. By believing in their ability to learn, grow, and develop, they are also creating the context for greater accomplishment and reaching their full potential.

CLOSED AND OPEN MINDSETS

Dweck's understanding of mindsets has powerful implications for our ability to connect with and learn from strangers. And it is a very useful framework for thinking about our own potential to innovate, find and engage the right people, collaborate and partner in more compelling ways, grow our enterprises, and lead. But let's tweak it just a bit. Instead of thinking about fixed and growth mindsets—which are certainly powerful ideas, substantiated by Dweck's extensive body of research on achievement and success—I'd like you to think about the notions of "closed" and "open" mindsets: mindsets more closely aligned with my focus on the necessity of strangers. The core characteristics of each are summarized as follows.

Understanding Closed and Open Mindsets

Closed Mindset	Open Mindset
With a closed mindset we are likely to believe that:	With an open mindset we are likely to believe that:
• We know best.	• We may not know best.
• There is a best way to do things.	• There are many ways to do things.
• Immediate results are valuable.	• Discovering possibilities is valuable.
• Having the right expertise is key.	• Having an open mind is essential.
• Internal brainstorming is the best way to come up with ideas.	• Engaging the world around us is the best way to come up with ideas.
• We should protect knowledge.	• We should share knowledge.
• People we know are important.	• Strangers are also important.

With a closed mindset, people and organizations believe that they know best and that there is almost always a single best way to address or solve any challenge. They are quick to focus on getting the task done and getting to the result, even when it limits their ability to create and compare meaningful alternatives. They are also more likely to believe in the power of expertise in solving any problem: find the right expert or experts, and they are halfway there. And if a problem does require new thinking, assign the usual suspects—that is, people they know best—to brainstorm as the best way to come up with new ideas. People and groups with a closed mindset also fail to see the value in regularly sharing knowledge with others. They are smart enough to come up with their own information and likely to protect or hoard it when they believe it gives them an advantage. And they are most likely to rely on people they already know and trust, or people like themselves, even when those people are not the most original thinkers and may have even gotten them into their current predicament. Strangers are to be avoided.

With an open mindset, people and organizations believe that they don't know everything and that they might not even know the best way to approach the challenges or opportunities they face. For them, the focus is on possibilities and how to come up with the best new product, service, solution, or customer experience based on clearly understanding the needs of those they are trying to serve. They may begin with some initial ideas, based on their own expertise, but they quickly solicit the input and perspectives of others, especially folks who look at the world in very different ways. In doing this, they are able to come to a better approach, one that might be a fusion of several ideas or ways of thinking. And in their efforts to gain knowledge they are also open to engaging strangers and sharing what they know. To them, knowledge is a way to collaborate with and be valuable to others.

It is useful to make a note about expertise, because its role in success carries a powerful weight in a closed mindset. Reliance on expertise is a hallmark of the cultures of many companies and organizations. This belief in its power is especially prevalent in organizations whose work demands a high level of technical or specialized knowledge, like professional service firms, engineering companies, IT companies, research agencies and think tanks, biotech and pharmaceutical firms, and so on. These are places filled with lots of highly trained technical people doing what they believe is highly technical work. And these people have invested a great deal of time, energy, training, and often money to become experts in their fields.

Over the years I have worked with many people who are truly geniuses in their chosen fields. But does that make them more likely to come up with breakthrough ideas? We assume that the answer to this question is a resounding "YES!" It is an assumption based on the belief—fostered by leading educational institutions, professional and scientific associations, and companies themselves—that the more we know about a specific area, the more likely we are to see its possibilities. *But what if this is not the case?* What if it turns out that the more we know about something, the less likely we are to see its possibilities and the more likely we are to see things as we have learned to rather than seeing how they could be?

Business success is all about seeing things in new ways and, as a result, creating new and more powerful solutions to the problems and opportunities we face. So although a high level of expertise is important and often essential, we are far more likely to create meaningful innovation when we combine what we know best with the ideas and expertise of others—especially if those ideas and that expertise are very different from our own. This curiosity and willingness to step outside of our comfort zones and beyond the bounds of our own expertise and knowledge make all the difference.

TESTING YOUR MINDSET

Here's a quick and energizing "test" that you can conduct to gauge whether you and your colleagues have a closed or an open mindset:

Divide people into groups of three to five and give each group a stack of roughly fifty paper dinner plates and fifty paper cups. Then give them three minutes to accomplish the following task, which you can write on a flipchart easel or a wall board:

Use the cups and plates to build the tallest tower possible.

That's it. Three minutes.

Here's what you are likely to find, if my experience with several hundred groups across a wide range of industries and cultures is any indication. Most people—that is, folks with a closed mindset—will quickly begin to use the cups and plates to build their towers in alternating rows of three cups, then one plate, followed by three more cups and another plate. And they'll do this until their tower starts to tilt and lose its form and balance. At that point they'll probably stop, because they've reached the limits of what is possible, given the materials at hand. After all, if cups and plates were really great building materials, we'd probably see a lot more of the world's buildings being made out of them.

Now, some groups will be more skillful than others in using the cups and plates to build relatively tall and relatively stable towers, especially if one or more of their members has had training as a structural engineer. But there is a limit to how tall their towers will be—roughly 72 inches, or 183 centimeters for those of you who use the slightly more rational metric system—and the group will eventually get stuck either before or after their paper tower falls to the ground.

So what's happened?

It turns out that the overwhelming majority of groups have actually added a word to the task—the word "only"—even though it wasn't part of their instructions. It was simply part of their DNA or mindset to define problems and opportunities as specifically as possible so they will be easier to handle. As a result, they actually tried to solve the following problem:

Use *only* the cups and plates to build the tallest tower possible.

And there's nothing wrong with doing it that way. It's just a way of thinking. They are simply focused on taking everything as a given in order to quickly get to the desired result of building the tallest tower. But this way of thinking is based on a closed mindset and has instantly limited their potential.

In the meantime, a small number of groups have thought about the task in a very different way, focusing instead on the objective of building the tallest tower and the word "possible." As a result, they were less preoccupied with the cups and plates and more focused on height. They didn't assume that the instruction prohibited them from using something other than the cups and plates, and they probably quickly realized that there were better ways to build a tall tower that included not just the cups and plates—like using a flipchart as a base, stacking chairs and notebooks on the table as a way to get started, having their tallest member stand on a table, or any number of other options for quickly gaining stable height. For them, anything was possible right from the start, as long as they met the minimum requirement of using some cups and plates. Their approach was based on a more open mindset.

Three minutes gives you a simple, though not totally scientific, starting point. If you would like a bit more insight and a way to start a meaningful conversation with your colleagues about different mindsets, you can also answer the following set of questions, based on the core characteristics described earlier.

Seven Questions to Help Us Understand Our Mindset

1. When faced with a new challenge, is your initial inclination to try to solve it by first applying the knowledge, approaches, and tools you already have?
2. When looking for people to collaborate with in solving a problem or creating a new opportunity, do you rely on people with backgrounds and expertise similar to your own?
3. Do you believe that there is generally a single best way to do something?
4. When trying to solve a problem, are you typically satisfied when you come up with an acceptable solution, or are you more likely to continue working until you get a more compelling result?

5. Do you make a regular practice of sharing the knowledge you develop or acquire with people outside your immediate group or team?

6. Do you believe that strangers—especially people in other, very different walks of life—have ideas, insight, and perspectives that could help you to solve the problems you face?

7. When faced with a problem or opportunity, are you very likely to search for solutions across a wide range of disciplines?

The best way to use these questions is to simply ask each member of your group or team to spend some time thinking about them and then write down his or her own candid answers. Then come together to share everyone's thoughts without passing judgment. This way introverts, extroverts, and the people in between will have an equal chance to have their ideas, perspectives, and voices heard. Next, use these initial answers as a starting point for a broader conversation about your goals and objectives, your real potential as a group—that is, what it would take to be remarkable—and the mindset required to reach your potential. Finally, share your ideas on concrete steps for moving forward—steps like taking a fresh look at the key challenges and opportunities you face, searching for possible solutions outside your comfort zone and areas of expertise, looking for more than one solution, sharing knowledge and ideas more consistently, and connecting with the right strangers from other walks of life.

■ ■ ■

The real value of these questions, and your commitment to answering them with candor, is their ability to spark a conversation about what it means to have an open mindset and why this really matters. In fact, this is the biggest challenge that separates us from reaching our full potential as individuals, companies, and organizations. Real success depends on being open to better ways of doing the things that matter most. Sometimes that means combining the best things that we know with the best things that other people know—and sometimes it means scrapping what we usually do in favor of an entirely new way of doing things. Here's an example: "cloud computing" has taken the world of business and government by storm as a game-changing alternative to buying our own software and maintaining our own data and all of our information resources. Instead, we can now hire a provider to take care of everything for us at a significantly lower cost, with fewer problems, and with greater quality and security—assuming we choose the right partner. But we have to be open to this new way of doing things.

In a growing number of industries, new business models are quickly becoming the order of the day, as strangers and others with equally open minds bring new and better perspectives to old and new marketplaces. We can't afford to have a closed mindset if we want to remain competitive in any business or walk of life. It is imperative that we figure out how to change our mindset.

FROM MINDSET TO GUIDING PRINCIPLES

To change our mindset, we will need a set of guiding principles or core values to support our openness to new people, ideas, and possibilities.

Guiding Principles for Building a More Open Mindset

- **Humility**—the belief that we don't know everything and that we can always be better at the things that matter most.
- **Curiosity**—our innate gift for being open to new ideas, new people, and new possibilities.

51

- **Respect**—the belief that everyone matters and that we learn and grow by engaging other people on their own terms.
- **Purpose**—our reason for being that guides our efforts to learn and grow.

Let's explore each of these guiding principles in turn.

Humility

It's hard to be open to new people and new ideas when we believe that *we* know the best way to do things, or that our expertise and worldview are better frameworks for solving problems, creating new opportunities, building organizations and teams, or serving customers. Not that we shouldn't be proud of what we know, but we should also appreciate the limits of our knowledge and the likelihood that there are even better ways to do the things that matter. Humility also means being genuinely interested in learning new things, making new connections, and understanding the value of different sources of inspiration. And it is not enough to be open to ideas at the margins of our world; we have to be open to thinking in new ways about the very heart of the work that we do—the areas central to our lives and work in which we have already made a major investment.

Humility means acknowledging and accepting that our expertise is not sufficient for many of the challenges we face. This is very difficult to do, because any big change is likely to put us back at the bottom of the learning curve. But in today's world we all have to commit to becoming nonstop and ever-faster learners. A good case in point is the world of pharmaceutical research and drug discovery. It is a world that used to be focused almost entirely on chemistry and built around legions of world-class researchers testing new compounds in the most sophisticated labs. But as new drug pipelines dried up, leading drug companies were forced to change their approach or at least to add some new paths to finding breakthrough products. These paths included mining the human genome for insight into new therapies that might apply to either large or more targeted groups of people. They also led to a renewed interest in understanding traditional medicines that have been developed and used by native people in some of the most remote parts of the world. As it turns out, a relatively large percentage of modern drugs have their origin in plants, but as our level of scientific knowledge and analytical expertise increased, drug companies lost their connection to rain forests, remote villages, and the less "expert" people who inhabit them. Now faced with the need to grow, they are returning to these roots with a new sense of humility and possibilities.

Curiosity

It's hard to build a more open mindset and stretch the bounds of what we are able to accomplish if we aren't curious about new people, ideas, and the world around us. We need to make cultivating and pursuing our curiosity a habit, part of the daily routine of our lives as individuals and organizations. Fortunately, we have a great precedent for doing this, because all of us were totally curious as children. Try to recall your own early childhood, when all you had to do was play, have fun, and engage the world head-on. Each day you explored your surroundings with a keen interest in discovering new things and figuring out how everything worked— examining trees to test their properties and communicate with their inhabitants, jumping enthusiastically in puddles to test basic tenets of hydrology, marveling at fire trucks as they raced by, and imagining a hundred uses for a ball. Then somewhere between the playground and the world of adult work—that is, in the course of school and more formal learning—most of us seemed to lose the knack for discovering new possibilities around us.

Now you need this innate ability more than ever. Imagine the smart folks at Levi Strauss, who created and patented the very first blue jeans in 1873. Levi Strauss has become one of the world's most famous and respected brands, selling a wide range of jeans and other clothes that epitomize a classic American style. But it is also a company that is still curious after 140 years and sends team members on travels around the world to find inspiration for new products, colors, clothes-making processes, and seasonal clothing collections. The company's innovation and success are based on curiosity and its people's ability to look beyond their own surroundings to engage and learn from strangers as a key to remaining new, current, and classic.

Being curious means being open to learning that might come from people who are very different from us, have very different interests from ours, do things in very different ways, and see the world very differently. To be truly curious, we have to broaden our interests and be open to insights from a much broader range of sources.

Respect

It's not enough to be humble and curious; we also need to have real respect for others and their knowledge, expertise, insights, culture, and worldview. To respect means to truly appreciate the value of what other people know and to seek to gain an understanding of the things they believe and hold dear. Regardless of whether a person has a very different educational background or no education at all; or the person is from a different discipline that seems to bear no relevant connection to the work we do and the lives we lead; or the person is from a different culture, with traditions, practices, and ways of looking at the world that seem very foreign; or the person is from a different generation and lives life in a very different way, the real challenge is to understand and appreciate the fact that all of these people know something that matters. And what they know could inform our work and lives in profound ways. Everyone is worth knowing, understanding, and valuing—from

Inuits to architects, teenagers to UPS drivers, Antarctic explorers to inventors, entrepreneurs to librarians, swimmers to local herbalists, hairdressers to automotive engineers, Muslim grandmothers to CEOs, and everyone in between.

In *You Can't Lead with Your Feet on the Desk*, Ed Fuller shares lessons from his career as the president of International Lodging for Marriott—a career in which he played a central role in helping this American hotel company to grow and become a leading and highly respected global brand.[6] This success was based on a clear and consistent belief in the importance of building strong personal relationships with people from different cultures and backgrounds. These relationships were based on gaining real understanding, learning to communicate, demonstrating respect, and building trust. In his worldview, when we respect other people—no matter how different they are from us—strangers can become lifelong friends, colleagues, and great partners.

Purpose

Purpose brings our open mindset to life. To really be interested in engaging and learning from other people, we need to be purposeful and to see making new connections with strangers and gaining new insight from them as a path to making a difference in something worth doing in our work or personal lives. This doesn't mean that we can't make new connections and learn new things just for the sake of learning. But it does suggest that having a compelling sense of purpose gives an importance and an urgency to connecting with strangers and cultivating an open mindset. It also suggests that we don't have to understand all of the details of what we are trying to accomplish. If we did, we probably would not be as open. Whether for an individual, a company, or an organization, focusing on a powerful reason for being helps to energize efforts to learn and grow. And when two or more people with a shared or related purpose meet, the opportunities to learn and understand become much more significant.

In 2000, I decided to start a nonprofit organization called Passion for Learning, Inc., for the purpose of helping at-risk children in our community to become passionate about learning (hence the name) and reach their full potential. But I didn't know exactly how to do it. All I really knew was that schools needed to make learning come alive and the community needed to show that it really cared about all of our kids. Our modest beginning was to invite people from all across the city to spend a day thinking about how all of our knowledge and resources could be brought to bear to inspire kids; through a bit of good luck and good timing, more than one hundred people came together to share their ideas around this simple purpose. These people were mostly strangers from all walks of life who believed in the promise of every child and who began to use their ideas, questions, insights, and creativity to make something happen. Today Passion for Learning is a small but thriving organization that has won awards for its innovative programs—programs that use digital literacy and the power of the written and spoken word to close the achievement gap and unlock the brilliance in all of our community's young people.

Sometimes our purpose may be relatively clear, but our path is created in large part by strangers.

CHANGING OUR BEHAVIOR

Let's take a moment to look at a set of simple behaviors that will help us cultivate a more open mindset. Let's also think about where we are today and how we can make a few changes that will make a real difference.

For many of us, our work lives are characterized by the following behaviors:

- Focusing on getting our work done
- Staying at our desks

- Relying on our expertise and the things we already know (because that's what we are being paid to do)
- Collaborating and brainstorming with people who are a lot like us
- Rarely looking beyond our walls for ideas and inspiration
- Avoiding, at almost all costs, stepping out of our comfort zones
- Avoiding people who are different from us

There's nothing wrong with any of these behaviors taken by themselves, but they are not likely to enable us to create real breakthroughs, find the best people, build more meaningful collaboration, gain new customers, or become better leaders. They are the living, breathing embodiment of a closed mindset and a guarantee that, if we stick with only these behaviors, we will lead only incrementally better work and personal lives.

Contrast these with the following set of behaviors—behaviors that we can and should be trying to incorporate in our everyday lives:

- Focusing on finding the real potential in our work
- Getting up and away from our desks to connect with colleagues in new ways and engage the world around us
- Acknowledging the strengths and limitations of our expertise and seeking to find new knowledge and approaches that will make us even more successful (because that's what we're really being paid to do)
- Seeking out opportunities to collaborate and brainstorm with people who are very different from us
- Consistently looking beyond our walls for ideas and inspiration
- Looking for opportunities to stretch outside our comfort zones
- Seeking to engage with strangers—especially if they are very different from us

These behaviors are the living, breathing embodiment of an open mindset and a guarantee that we will be more open to reaching our full potential.

Realize that our openness to new people, ideas, and possibilities is something we can develop over time. In fact, we can continue to develop it over our entire lives and careers as we turn new behaviors into consistent habits. Think about all of the ways that you have become more open over the years, paying particular attention to the types of people, experiences, and sources of information for which you now have a greater appreciation. Although many people believe that they become less open to new things over time and more set in their ways, my experience working with more than three hundred companies and organizations is quite the opposite. The biggest challenge is getting people and organizations to be willing to take the first step—a step that is often as easy as getting up and taking a walk with their eyes wide open.

Since 2003, I have begun many assignments by teaching our customers to do exactly that through a process we call "Team Learning Adventures." At the core of this process is a simple and energizing exploration of the world beyond our workplaces, in which visits to other businesses, museums, neighborhoods, schools, restaurants, and artistic performances become an invitation to rediscover our innate gift of curiosity and the value of being open to new people, places, ideas, and perspectives. And a chance to discover the real power of strangers from all walks for life—strangers who are vital to our success in almost anything that matters.

Now let's see how to put an open mindset and these behaviors into practice in the real world of business and the rest of our lives.

PART TWO

Practice

FOUR

Innovation

You cannot discover new oceans unless you have the
courage to lose sight of the shore.
—ANDRÉ GIDE

We all know that *innovation* is essential to the success of companies, organizations, and individuals. If they are to grow and prosper, enterprises of all types and sizes must continually deliver even greater value to the people and businesses they have the privilege to serve. And they do this by innovating, in order to:

- Develop better products, services, and solutions
- Create more remarkable and more valuable customer experiences
- Improve the quality and efficiency of the ways they produce and distribute their offerings

Otherwise, they run the risk of becoming less relevant.

Most companies and organizations seem to understand this—at least conceptually—because they spend an awful lot of time and energy talking about innovation and touting its importance in their board and shareholder meetings; on their websites; and in their marketing materials, business proposals, and job postings. Many have even put considerable resources behind their efforts to be more innovative by creating a more supportive business culture and mindset. They have made investments in research and development, created focused innovation initiatives and even innovation centers, provided training to employees at all levels, and tried to figure out what incentives will spark the new ideas that can drive improvements in top- and bottom-line performance. They do this because they know that if they don't figure out better ways of doing the things that matter most, and they don't build the right mindset to become more open and adaptable, they simply won't be able to compete. The same companies and organizations that need to innovate consistently also need employees who can drive, or at least implement, innovation. They need people who can provide them with new ways of thinking and help them take action.

Having said this, most of us are stuck with a very strange notion of how innovation happens, which severely constrains our potential and our innate ability to be brilliant when it matters. It's a notion that is built around the power of smart people *putting their heads together*. When you ask most companies and organizations how they innovate or come up with powerful new ideas, they quickly say that they spend a lot of time encouraging their sharpest minds to spend time brainstorming, and that brainstorming and innovative thinking are core competencies. They often add that they have created meeting places designed specifically for innovation, with floor-to-ceiling whiteboards and more flexible arrangements that enable people to stretch their thinking. They might also note that they regularly send teams to the finest offsite retreat facilities, where, freed from the constraints of day-to-day business and a boatload of limiting rules and requirements, they can let their imaginations and creativity run wild. Imaginations fueled by clever people working together and combining their expertise, experience, and insights.

Sounds like a winning combination, doesn't it?

If only it were so simple. What is emerging as common practice flies in the face of not only reality, but the entire history of innovation—a history built on the ability of people, working on their own and in groups, to get beyond the limits of their own expertise, experience, and insights and beyond what they know best. To get up off of their individual and collective bottoms in a search for new ideas, insights, and perspectives that can really spark their creativity. To leave the confines of even the hippest and best-designed meeting room in order to engage the world head-on with a compelling sense of openness, wonder, honesty, and possibilities. To seek inspiration by exploring the ideas and insights of others—around the corner and around the planet. To connect with strangers toiling in similar fields but in different ways and with strangers in different fields who know things they don't know, so they can combine this new learning—and, more important, understanding—with the things they know best.

Innovation is a quest to be different in ways that matter, rather than a task to create a slightly newer version of what we already do.

But even our words give away our lack of understanding. Doesn't it strike you as a bit odd that we would have a "retreat" in order to innovate? Yet that is exactly what most companies and organizations decide to do when faced with the challenge of coming up with new ideas and better ways of thinking. They organize a retreat. Wouldn't we get off to a much better start if we used words that connote progress instead of moving backward, and if we invited people to an "advance," or a "forward," or a fresh look "ahead," or even a "happening"?

But that's only half of the problem, because we often decide that a key to innovation is getting away from everything and finding a quiet and peaceful place where there won't be any distractions. Even though innovation is *all about being distracted*—distracted from the way we normally think about things. We'd actually be much better off if we held our advance, forward, ahead, or happening in the middle of a big, bustling, and chaotic city in a world filled with possibilities.

Consider this fact:

Ninety-nine percent of all new ideas are based on *an idea or practice that someone or something else has already had.*

If that isn't a call to engage strangers, then I don't know what is. Yet most of us, when challenged to think "outside the box" in order to solve a pressing problem or create an important new business opportunity, seem content to rack our brains trying to come up with our own original idea. Is it any wonder that most people don't believe they are creative? Or that most organizations are convinced that there is a small subset of people in their ranks who are innovative by nature and uniquely qualified to come up with brilliant ideas? This kind of thinking allows the rest of us to simply plod along, doing the best we can, and absolves us of having to take initiative and make a difference. And it is not only limiting, but also wrong.

We all have the potential to be innovative and brilliant. But we won't fulfill it if we, and the places we work in, don't change our mindset and our game. The good news is we can.

And strangers are the real key to our success.

HELICOPTERS, HAIRSTYLES, AND CARS THAT WON'T COLLIDE

Everyone knows who invented the light bulb, the telephone, the airplane, and the iPad. That would be the collaborative and customer-focused Thomas Edison (*kinda sorta*—he was actually building on an idea that was more than fifty years old); the intellectually curious and intense Alexander Graham Bell (*kinda sorta*—he was actually relying on a series of insights on electrical transmission that began with the work of Carl Friedrich Gauss and Wilhelm Eduard Weber in 1833); the passionate and persistent Wright Brothers (*kinda sorta*—they based their thinking on some other less notable successes and failures in powered flight); and Steve Jobs (again, *kinda sorta*—he probably had a bit of help from other folks at Apple, not to mention the history of tablet computers, which, amazingly, got their start in 1888).

But we still have these wonderful notions of Edison in his lab in Menlo Park; Bell making his first call to his assistant Thomas Watson; Orville and Wilbur on the beach at Kitty Hawk, North Carolina; and Jobs on stage in his blue jeans and black turtleneck showing us Apple's latest life-changing device. And that's okay. Innovators deserve credit for being smart enough to build on the knowledge of strangers.

Now, let me ask you: Who invented the helicopter? This is a flying machine as remarkable as the airplane, with the unique ability to take off vertically, hover over almost any place, then zoom forward, stop, and come straight down. An awe-inspiring contraption with all kinds of cool uses that range from helping on the battlefield, to assisting in medical emergencies, to rescuing people and transporting supplies in and out of the most difficult-to-reach places, to reporting on traffic tie-ups during our morning and evening commutes, to shuttling presidents and other dignitaries to meetings and airports. But it's a question that only a few people know the answer to.

In fact, there probably isn't one inventor of the helicopter. The honor would likely be shared by a number of people. But the person who is now given the most credit for the commercialization of the helicopter is Igor Sikorsky, a Russian immigrant to the United States. His brilliance and determination as an innovator exemplify the necessity of strangers in our success.

Sikorsky grew up in Kiev in the late 1800s; from an early age, he had a keen interest in flight and the emerging field of aeronautics. He learned about the Wright Brothers and their flying machine during a visit to Germany and also marveled at the ideas of a curious fellow named Count Ferdinand von Zeppelin. The Count was working on a "lighter than air" aircraft—what became known as the "zeppelin"—that could lift straight up from the ground, then literally float, with a bit of power, to its destination. But unlike a balloon, von Zeppelin's aircraft had an engine and could be easily guided in the direction of its pilot's choosing. For a very short while zeppelins were the most reliable means of long-distance passenger travel. That is, of course, until the disastrous crash of the Hindenburg in 1937. But to someone like Sikorsky they must have been a most profound inspiration. So much so that after studying in Paris he returned to Kiev to try to build a helicopter.

The project failed initially and led him back to the world of airplanes. And even though his first attempt to build an airplane also failed, by 1912—just nine years after the Wright Brothers had flown for an amazing fifty-nine seconds—Sikorsky was designing planes that stayed airborne for more than an hour and that were used eventually as bombers in World War I. When the Russian Revolution ended his career in Russia, Sikorsky moved to France to look for work. But, unable to find a suitable job in the budding aviation industry there, in 1919 he immigrated to the United States, where he established the Sikorsky Aero Engineering Corporation. At the start of this venture the corporation designed and built a progression of successful airplanes before turning its attention to Sikorsky's real passion, helicopters.

But it wasn't simply the Wright Brothers and the count who inspired and guided Sikorsky. No, it's probably safe to say that the notion of a helicopter came into existence at least two thousand years earlier, when the Chinese invented a propeller, put it on a stick, and created a toy known as a "Chinese Top" that could *fly* straight up when the stick was spun quickly. It's a toy that can still be found in many toy stores around the world. And it's probable that, like most of us, Sikorsky was familiar with Leonardo Da Vinci's famous drawing of an "ornithopter flying machine" or "aerial screw" in which human power is used to compress air and create vertical flight. But we can only imagine that Da Vinci, a rather clever guy who was also a particularly keen observer of the world around him, might have himself been inspired by things he saw on walks outside his home in Florence. Specifically, dragonflies—those amazing little creatures with a remarkable gift for flight that includes being able to stop in mid-air, zoom into a flower, and then fly backward at full speed. The flying backward quickly part is something that still defies modern technology.

And there were other sources of insight on the journey to Sikorsky's grand invention. These included the French naturalist Christian de Launoy and his colleague Bienvenue, who in 1784 created a rotary-winged toy that could actually lift straight up and fly. Shortly after that, in 1796, an Englishman, Sir George Cayley, built a model helicopter driven by elastic bands. Another Englishman, W. H. Phillips, constructed a large steam-driven model helicopter in 1842; this was followed by another steam-driven model designed in 1878 by an Italian engineer, Enrico Forlanini. Even Thomas Edison experimented with the idea of vertical flight in the 1880s.

It wasn't until 1907, however, that French engineer Paul Cornu invented the first helicopter with a pilot on board. He was the pilot— likely the only person crazy enough to give it a try—and his initial flight lasted only twenty seconds, at a height of roughly one foot or thirty centimeters off the ground. It was indeed a start, though after a few tweaks and a few more attempts Cornu abandoned his efforts to refine his invention.

Clearly Sikorsky knew, from the history of strangers, that vertical flight was indeed possible. So finally, in 1939, his VS-300 launched, becoming the first viable helicopter, and in May 1941 an improved version of the VS-300 set an international flight record of more than an hour in continuous flight. This innovation was driven by the ideas, insights, drawings, toys, and experiments of a world of others trying to solve the very same challenge—others who happened to be strangers to each other.

Sometimes inspiration comes from a completely different field or walk of life.

Reinventing Style

Vidal Sassoon never intended to revolutionize the world of fashion and hair design, and he might not have, except for circumstance and the fact that he was open to the power of learning from strangers in other disciplines. Sassoon grew up in poverty in East London, and his real interest was in fighting racial hatred and the fascist gangs that surfaced in England after the end of World War II. But, given his family's economic situation, when Sassoon was fourteen his mother apprenticed him to a local barbershop. Although this was not something that Sassoon had shown any interest in, he committed himself to becoming the very best hairdresser possible, and he decided that the best way to make this happen would be to work for London's richest, most successful, and most fashion-savvy people. To this end, he decided to regularly attend the theater, where he would learn how to speak "posh" English as his ticket to finding work in London's West End. There he would have the opportunity to "toil over the finest heads of hair by day" and then head out to the streets at night to fight injustice.[1] But in 1948 a slight detour took him from London to the new state of Israel. He would eventually return to open his own hair salon on fashionable Bond Street, but having taken that detour from the world he knew would spark his greatest innovation.

After his return to London, for nine years Sassoon experimented with a range of new and unique hairstyles and techniques, with a keen focus on creating simple and elegant looks for his clients. His claim to fame came in 1963, when he created the "Bob and Five-Point Cut," also known simply as the "Bob." It was a revolutionary hairstyle that quickly caught on and earned him renown as the "founder of modern hairdressing."[2] And it became a style that still endures, fifty years later—which is not too shabby or shaggy. Vidal Sassoon went on to leverage his fame by partnering with hair salons across the United Kingdom and the United States and by developing a very popular line of hair care products that continues to be sold throughout the world today.

But what is most interesting about this remarkable innovator is the source of his inspiration and vision, because it didn't come from going to classes or from watching other leading hairdressers in the top salons of London. Rather, his real breakthrough came from studying Bauhaus architecture and design—an innovative architectural and arts movement that began in Germany just after World War I. Bauhaus had its roots in the cultural movement of Modernism, which focused on simple forms, functionality, and the hopeful idea of producing significant buildings, crafts, and arts for the masses.

As Bauhaus design focused on simple geometric shapes and sharp angles, so too did Sassoon's hair designs. His new looks were short and often strikingly simple, with a geometry that mirrored his clients' facial structure. The renowned German-American architect Ludwig Mies van der Rohe, one of the leading figures of both Bauhaus and modern architecture, used the phrase "less is more"[3] to summarize this new view of design, and it was clear that Sassoon found new inspiration in the possibility of creating hairstyles that were "less" and "more" at the same time—easy to cut, easy to take care of, simple, functional, accessible to everyone, stylish, and, as it turned out, viewed as the new sexy. These were haircuts that women could wash at home and then wear with little or no maintenance, and Sassoon created them at a time when the traditional world of hair design was one of complicated styles that were stiff and typically required women to either use hair curlers and hairspray or visit the beauty salon every week. His innovation came from studying the genius of strangers whose work he saw in the streets and shops of northern Europe and in the emerging cityscape of modern Israel—especially Tel Aviv, which was becoming a center of Bauhaus design during his sojourn there.

When Sassoon died in 2012, Grace Coddington, creative director of *Vogue* magazine, said that Sassoon had "changed the way everyone looked at hair."[4] And isn't this what innovation is really all about? Changing the way that people look at a product, a service, a solution, an industry, an aspect of life, a style, or the way that things are done? By being open to the world around him and inspired by strangers who were doing the very same thing in a very different field, Sassoon found his inspiration and innovation. He was inspired by the fields of architecture and design, not by asking friends in the world of hairdressing for their ideas.

This can be true for all of us. By changing the way people look at hair, or clothes, or communication, or hospitality, or information technology, or government contracting, or health care, or transportation, or education, or food, or anything else worth doing, we have real power to innovate. And the key is often thinking based on very different ideas and a very different frame of reference.

It is interesting to note that Walter Isaacson, in his biography of Steve Jobs, writes that this visionary was also "heavily influenced by the Bauhaus movement."[5] Further proof that simple is compelling and that innovation can be simpler than we imagine in a world filled with strangers.

Learning from a Different Kind of School

And sometimes inspiration doesn't even come from humans. In 2009 Nissan Motors caused a stir in the world of automotive engineering by announcing that it was developing technology that would prevent cars from colliding with each other by enabling them to maintain a "uniform distance of separation" under any driving conditions.[6] It was an exciting idea—unless, of course, you happened to own an auto body shop—and it was based on a challenge that many leading automotive engineers had been wrestling with for several decades without any major breakthroughs. Sure, today's vehicles, especially high-end cars, have an interesting and growing array of sensors that enable them to detect other vehicles, large stationary objects, deer, lane markings, median barriers, and even pedestrians. And these sensors are likely to improve over time with advances in technology. But avoiding other moving objects? That's pretty cool.

What made Nissan's announcement more intriguing was the source of the company's inspiration. They literally went back to "school" to rethink this technical problem. Or, more accurately, back to "schools"—schools of fish, that is. Large schools of fish are able to swim continuously in very crowded places—making nearly instantaneous starts, stops, and changes in direction without ever colliding. In fact, a quick bit of research suggests that there have never been any recorded cases of massive fish crashes or pile-ups in any of the world's oceans, lakes, or rivers.

According to Nissan, "Fish recognize their surroundings based on lateral-line sense and sense of sight and form schools based on three behavior rules."[7] These rules are:

1. *Collision avoidance*—Fish are able to change direction without colliding with each other or other obstacles that are in their way.
2. *Traveling side by side*—Fish are able to travel next to each other while keeping a certain distance between them and matching each other's speed.
3. *Approaching*—Fish are able to gain closer proximity to other fish that are at a distance from them.

All of this is based on an uncanny ability to communicate continuously. An ability that Nissan decided to program into a robotic car called the "EPORO"—a car that the company envisions as the prototype for a new generation of real, highly efficient collision-avoiding vehicles.

According to Toshiyuki Andou, manager of the Nissan Mobility Laboratory in Japan and principal engineer of the project, "We recreated the behavior of a school of fish making full use of cutting-edge electronic technologies. By sharing the surrounding information received within the group via communication, the group of EPOROs can travel safely, changing its shape as needed."[8] Remember, innovation occurs when we combine what we know with the ideas, experiences, and wisdom of others. Sometimes those others don't even need to be human. In this instance, it was fish, and the marine biologists who understand them best—not the usual suspects in the quest to solve a tricky automotive engineering problem. But in this case and in a world in which we are open to the possibilities presented by other people and creatures with insight to share, fish are logical partners.

Building on Several Inspirations

Even Apple, viewed by many as one of the most innovative and original companies in the world, owes much of its great success to the ideas of strangers. Think about what makes the iPod media player, with its 70 percent market share, so ubiquitous and successful. Certainly design, ease of use, and functionality have a lot to do with it. But Apple didn't invent the concept of personalized music—that was Sony, in 1979, with its then-revolutionary Walkman.[9] And Apple didn't invent the technology platform the iPod relies on—that was audio engineer Karlheinz Brandenburg and a German company named Fraunhofer-Gesellshaft, which developed the MP3 standard and received a patent for it in 1989.[10] Ten years later, the first portable MP3 players hit the market, two years before the first iPod. And Apple, with its wildly successful iTunes store, certainly didn't invent the notion of creating the greatest single source of content in the world; that was the Egyptians, who roughly 2,300 years ago built the great library of Alexandria—a library that contained more than four hundred thousand documents long before there were printing presses. What Apple did was combine its own brilliance with these inputs from strangers, along with the skills of a number of equally clever outside partners, to create the most compelling offering and product ecosystem available.

FROM 3M To 3-D AND BEYOND

From the middle of 1970s until the late 1990s, 3M emerged as one of the world's most innovative companies. With its special mix of knowledge, talent, technological expertise, and culture, the company became an unrivaled innovation engine that was the envy of the media, leading business thinkers, and other companies across a wide range of industries that would journey to 3M's headquarters in St. Paul, Minnesota, to learn its "secrets."

There was good reason to believe that culture was really what set 3M apart from its competitors.[11] 3M's culture was based on a commitment to enabling employees to look beyond their jobs and devote 15 percent of their time to working on their own ideas and projects. This approach helped the company develop a string of successful ideas and new products that transformed its performance and offered an encouraging model for other companies trying to innovate more consistently. 3M's innovations include the now-famous Post-it note, which made Art Fry, the creator, something of an industrial and business rock star—all because he had the modest notion that he could apply a unique adhesive, developed years earlier by colleague Spencer Silver, to a bookmark that would stay in place, then easily lift off. What made the notion even more modest was his initial thought to use these notes in his church hymnal so he could follow along with the service as he sang in the choir.

Making Room for Serendipity

3M actually started its "15 percent" program in 1948, applying the idea to every one of its employees based on the simple logic that innovation was essential to ongoing success and that anyone in the organization had the potential to come up with a new and powerful idea if given the time to think and explore. And although employees were, and still are, free to work on almost anything, most of the ideas that have been developed have come from projects done inside the company sparked in the normal course of business and through new collaborations with colleagues in different parts of the organization. Often these colleagues are relative strangers.

It is a process that, even in the early years, resulted in a somewhat steady stream of game-changing and industry-leading discoveries. Discoveries like Scotchgard, the amazing fabric protector. Simply spray it on your favorite carpet, cloth sofa, or winter coat and the most disgusting dirt, grime, and slime will refuse to stick. One might imagine that this "miracle" of modern science and technology was created deliberately in a world-class lab by a team of highly focused experts, who happened to be driven by the promise of protecting fabric and furniture. But, in fact, it was created by an accidental collaboration.

In 1952 a 3M employee named Patsy Sherman was working on a very different challenge—conducting experiments on fluorochemical polymers that would resist deterioration from jet aircraft fuels. Unfortunately, her best efforts at the time were failing. But one day, one of the assistants in her lab accidentally spilled a few drops of an experimental compound on her tennis shoes, and it became impossible to remove. Sherman was curious about the resiliency of this compound and, with help from another 3M chemist named Sam Smith, began to think about the possibility of creating a polymer that could actually repel oil and water from fabric to create a barrier against stains.

Innovation is a funny business. We know that focus is important, but we also know that it isn't always enough. Serendipity matters too. And colleagues and collaborators are important, but strangers also matter, both inside and outside our organizations—strangers with new ideas, interests, and approaches, and their own slime-resistant possibilities.

Other innovations from 3M's policy of openness have included masking tape; Scotch tape; Thinsulate—the semi-amazing insulating material that makes gloves, coats, hats, shoes, and pants and the people who wear them warmer in cold weather; as well as Cubitron, a unique sandpaper that acts more like a cutting tool.

But the thought of giving people time to explore and work on anything of interest, and the belief in the potential brilliance of every employee—not just leading scientists and technical people—must have seemed like totally radical ideas in 1948. In fact, they are still totally radical ideas for most companies today, with the exception of places like Google, which gives its employees 20 percent of their time to work on their own ideas and projects.

Yet by 2000, 3M was losing its groove. That's when James McNerney, a highly regarded executive from General Electric, was brought into the company with a plan to change the culture based on his experience with GE's successful Six Sigma program. His approach was to focus on improving business efficiencies and product quality in an organization that seemed to some people, and in particular to Wall Street, to lack basic business discipline. For a while, at least, this change in direction seemed to work, and 3M's stock rose significantly. But this approach also seemed to undermine the heart of a business that had been built more on the power of imagination and possibilities than on rigorous adherence to processes.[12] And with this change, 3M began to drop in the ranks of the most innovative companies.

McNerney left after five years to become the head of Boeing, and a new leadership team at 3M sought to strike a greater balance between creativity and process discipline. Several years later, it remains unclear whether the company can regain its place as a world-class innovator in a world in which new competitors, changing customer needs, and an even faster pace of technological change make it even more imperative to be externally focused.

An Invitation to Collaborate

Now imagine that an entirely new industry can be born based on the creativity, energy, and collaboration of strangers—that's just what happens in the fascinating world of 3-D printing. If you're not familiar with the concept, let me put it in very simple terms. Imagine being able to use your office printer to create three-dimensional objects like model cars, furniture for doll houses, repair parts for household appliances and industrial machines, toy robots, or pro-totypes for anything from shoes and handbags to aircraft, based on any idea that can be imagined, designed, and captured on a computer screen, which is then "produced" in minutes rather than days or months.

In an era of rapid prototyping and new product development, in which more and more companies are realizing the benefits of creating a very rough first draft of an idea (also known as a "minimally viable product" or "MVP") to test with customers before making a big investment, 3-D printing is a real breakthrough in the science and art of innovation. This breakthrough is all about creating a new business model by empowering a world filled with strangers to unlock and share their creativity, because 3-D printing has the potential to enable a world of trained and untrained designers and innovators to address challenges and opportunities that have three-dimensional solutions at a fraction of the cost and time required by traditional approaches to design and new product development. Coupled with innovations in social media, it is also a powerful invitation to collaborate in new ways.

It's also useful to think about the power of social media as a primary driver of innovation today—but not simply in terms of its ability to connect us with more people or spread the word about a new product, service, or solution. The Web provides a great way for companies and organizations of all shapes and sizes to stand out from the pack by being different in ways that really matter.

Bringing Old and New Technology Together

Let's play word association to give you a sense of what I mean. When I say "YouTube," what are the first things that come to mind? If you are like most people, including our teenage kids and their friends, you will probably think about videos, music, entertainment, advertising, networking, self-expression, and even self-promotion. You might also think about way too many adorable and at times amusing films about puppies, kittens, otters holding hands, and other animals doing decidedly human sorts of things. But what are the chances that you quickly thought of appliance parts? It's probably a number approaching zero, unless you happen to work for a Michigan company called RepairClinic. It's a company that simply sells replacement parts for a wide range of common household appliances and does it better than anyone else. There's nothing particularly innovative or remarkable about that. Except there is. A big part of their success is tied to YouTube, because they have figured out how to turn this popular website into a powerful customer service and education tool. In fact, at the time of this writing, RepairClinic has uploaded more than one thousand YouTube videos on topics ranging from repairing your refrigerator's ice-maker, to changing your lawn mower blade, to replacing the agitator in your washing machine without getting agitated. All are done simply and professionally by regular people we can all relate to, and all of these videos are intended for the vast majority of customers who don't own a tool belt. Since launching its YouTube "channel" in 2010, its how-to videos have been viewed more than 13.5 million times.

With RepairClinic videos being watched more than twenty thousand times a day, the company has created a powerful formula for adding real value to a commodity business in which most people are buying more and more products online. This happened because someone looked at the world and imagined that the right products, a fair price, fast delivery, and an increasingly popular technology could be combined to deliver more compelling and enabling value to a market of do-it-yourself customers—in a decidedly old-technology business.

Innovation is all about connecting with, learning from, collaborating with, and empowering strangers.

FINDING THE RIGHT STRANGERS

Once we understand that strangers are a necessity in innovation, the very nature of how we attempt to come up with new ideas changes dramatically. Instead of locking ourselves in a room and racking our brains until we create entirely new possibilities, we unlock ourselves from our desks and the ways of thinking that tend to limit our ability to create real breakthroughs. We can then begin to imagine a world filled with people and places that might stir our creativity or hold the missing piece or pieces to the puzzle we are trying to solve. In other words, we challenge ourselves to figure out who the perfect strangers are—the folks who understand important things we don't, or the folks who have developed new business models that could be used to reinvent our world, or for whom our "gaps" are second nature. Sometimes these strangers are close by; other times they are likely to be in industries or walks of life that are, at first blush, beyond our understanding and our reach.

Sometimes the right strangers are colleagues working down the hall or in another location of our own company or organization. Folks we may have passed by in the lunch room or seen at an all-hands meeting but never found the time to connect with in order to learn more about who they are, what they do, what they know, and, most important, what they are passionate about. We have simply never had the occasion or never imagined that they might help us to solve the challenges or opportunities we face.

And sometimes the right strangers are outside our enterprise but right under our noses, and we simply fail to notice them, like with the curious case of the Census Bureau and its quest to create a handheld device. If we are not willing to find and open to finding the perfect stranger to support our objectives, we are missing the real nature of innovation.

No matter how wonderful our best thinking is, we all have limitations. Yet in our rush to be brilliant and make something happen, we fail to open our eyes to a world of possibilities and instead rely on our own understanding of the best way to innovate, rather than exploring a new framework or perspective. But what if we could unlock a lot more brainpower? Wouldn't we have a significantly better chance of coming up with a real breakthrough?

The answer to tapping more brainpower lies in our willingness and ability to learn to cast a much wider net, and it is vital to building the mindset we discussed. This "wider net" might begin with the expertise of those around us—including our colleagues and the "usual suspects" of partners—but it also gives us the chance to look into other domains that have relevant insight to share. In working with our customers as they seek to broaden their thinking, I've developed a simple tool and thought process to guide this type of essential inquiry—a thought process that enables us to quickly gain access to a lot more creativity and brainpower than we ever imagined, by trying to imagine where insight might come from and organizing the world based on a more open mindset. This way we aren't constrained in our search for the kinds of ideas that really matter and that could create much greater value for those we serve.

Figure 4.1 depicts this straightforward idea of casting a wider net. I call it the Universe of Possibilities, though that title may be a bit of a stretch, as the universe is pretty big and especially difficult to depict on a single page. And so is a galaxy, so the picture really looks a lot more like a solar system, with your challenge or opportunity represented by the sun and circled by eight "domains" (or planets) where you can seek to discover new ideas and possibilities. This also aligns nicely with the eight planets that are now in our solar system—given that our childhood friend Pluto was demoted to dwarf planet status in 2006.

Figure 4.1 The Universe of Possibilities

Here's how it works.

For each important challenge or opportunity you and your colleagues face, try to stretch your thinking by looking at it from the following perspectives:

1. *What's our best thinking to date?* Not just in our immediate team, group, or business unit, but in the wealth of knowledge and insight that resides all across our company or organization.

2. *What's the best thinking in our industry?* Not just in our company, even if we are an industry leader, but also in the wisdom of our leading competitors and partners. It is useful to know their best thinking, because it might give us a better starting point for innovating and understanding what is possible within a world that we are still quite familiar with.

Let me pause for a second here to suggest that this is typically about as far as most companies and organizations go in their quest to think differently. Although it is a legitimate start to looking beyond the confines of our own walls, it doesn't really stretch our thinking very far unless we are way behind the curve, and I believe we all have the ability to do a lot better. So let's keep going.

3. *What's the best thinking in other industries?* Not just in our industry, but in other industries that are renowned for their genius in meeting the challenges and opportunities that we face. These can be industries that we are somewhat familiar with or very different industries with different offerings and different types of customers. The key here is to figure out who is simply brilliant and innovative at something that could change our world, whether it is customer service, new product development, the use of social media as a marketing tool, engaging employees, software as a service, distribution, or anything else that could be part of our equation for being remarkable.

4. *What's the best thinking from popular culture?* Not just in the world of business, but also in other walks of life where new ideas and approaches have changed the way things are done. What do artists and performers know about getting and captivating an audience? What do the world's finest chefs—folks like Alice Waters of Chez Panisse in Berkeley, California, and René Redzepi of Noma in Copenhagen, Denmark—understand about creating meaning and evoking emotion? What do teenagers know about lifestyle and getting the most value out of technology? I can tell you this much: anyone who makes a living writing operating manuals for consumer electronics products had better start looking for a new line of work. Today, young people simply open the box, throw away the instructions, and instantly start to use their devices with far greater skill than the rest of us.

5. *What's the best thinking in other cultures?* Not just in our culture, but in a bigger world filled with fresh and exciting ideas, perspectives, and insights. Now we will really have to test our evolving sense of openness by suggesting that for many of the challenges and opportunities we face, the best insight may come from other cultures where they have different ways of looking at the world. Ever stop to think about what micro lenders in South Asia might know about sparking innovation? Or what sumo wrestlers in Japan might know about competition? Or what the daring and creative members of the

French Canadian entertainment company Cirque du Soleil might know about how to fuse ideas from a variety of cultural traditions into a much more remarkable whole?

6. *What's the best insight from nature?* Not just in the domain of humans, though we are a relatively clever species, but also in the amazing workings of the rest of the natural world, with all of its creatures, systems, and wisdom. We saw how fish inspired automotive engineers and hummingbirds suggested the possibility of vertical flight. And that's just the tip of the iceberg. Nature abounds with best practices, from the burrs that inspired Velcro to different forms of communication and very natural networks that have widespread implications for how we work together and connect with customers.

7. *What's the best insight from science?* Not just in the realm of our work and its theories, but also in the brilliance of leading scientific minds in all disciplines. Just for fun, take an afternoon to learn more about the history of scientific discovery and some of the latest breakthroughs in fields near to and far from the work that you do. You might even enjoy learning the stories behind the latest Nobel Prize winners in scientific fields, because their discoveries and their thought processes could offer you a new perspective on your world and the challenges you face.

8. *What are the best possibilities from science fiction?* Not just from our view of reality, but also from all of the visions of others who have imagined a future filled with very different possibilities. And here is a chance to let your curiosity and creativity take flight, because science fiction is all about innovation, and you and your colleagues are free to invent a much more remarkable world when it comes to the products, services, solutions, and experience you offer.

And how might all of these perspectives fit together? That's for you to decide, because there could be several sources of inspiration.

Let's say you are interested in rethinking corporate education and designing a new learning program that truly engages and inspires all of your people. You could definitely begin by looking at the most successful corporate education programs that might have real insight into meeting your challenge. But you could also look at the changing world of colleges and universities, not just here but in other parts of the world; or the exemplary methods of the Finnish national educational system; or the remarkable success of Khan Academy and TED conferences as ways to train and inspire people. You might even look at how mothers and fathers of other species quickly teach their young enough to head out on their own, or what neuroscientists have discovered about learning, or how people in invented worlds have envisioned the learning process and the act of gaining new knowledge.

It is all fertile ground for stretching our thinking about how to be more valuable and more remarkable. And all based on our ability to get comfortable with the notion that the path to innovation and success has a lot to do with strangers.

Realize, too, that sometimes we can be inspired by simply getting up and out and walking around without a predetermined destination in mind, by simply being open to anything that might cross our path—a person, a business, an exhibit at a local museum, a lunchtime performance in a local park, or something we find in nature. At other times, we are free to choose a destination and to make a connection with a specific person or organization, or a set of ideas that begin to fill our gaps, and all we really need is an open mind and a pair of comfortable shoes to unlock our real potential.

And if you are looking for a place to get started, or a starting point for challenging the people in your organization, you can always begin with the simple notion of figuring out how to become the entrepreneur of your job or areas of responsibility. Let the broad universe around you fill you with inspiration and possibilities about how to reinvent what you do every day.

Innovation is imperative for companies, organizations, and individuals as they try to compete and succeed in a world that is constantly changing and that places a premium on new ideas, new offerings, and new ways of doing the things that matter most. But all too often they miss the mark in understanding where the best ideas come from and, as a result, limit their ability to think and act in more compelling ways. Although innovation isn't easy, we do know that the most innovative people and enterprises have a greater openness to the world around them and a greater willingness to cast a wider net and learn from strangers. This should be part of the formula that all of us follow.

People

*Only those who risk going too far can possibly
find out how far one can go.*
—T. S. ELIOT

We all know that having the right people is vital to the success of companies and organizations. In order to grow and prosper, enterprises of all types and sizes must continually attract, retain, and motivate employees and leaders at all levels with the skills to create and deliver winning products, services, solutions, and customer experiences. We also know that having the right skills is key to our personal success at work and in other aspects of our lives. So it's not surprising that most corporate, government, and nonprofit websites, annual reports, ads, blogs, Facebook pages, and job postings go out of their way to highlight the importance of people.

Here are some statements taken directly from leading companies in the United States and around the world that will give a quick sense of their belief in the value of their people:

"Our people are our greatest asset."
"Our people are our single greatest strength."
"Our people are great!"

"Our people are at the heart of our business strategy and success."

"Our people are the most innovative, intelligent and dynamic in our
industry."

"Our people are the best in our industry."

"Our people are the most knowledgeable and dedicated in the world."

"Our people are the best trained and they like what they do."

"Our people are the most creative and innovative thinkers."

"Our people go above and beyond."

"Our people go that extra mile."[1]

Quite simply, our people rock! It is enough to make a grown man
or woman cry tears of joy. If I'm an employee, it must be reassuring to
know that I am so highly valued—even if my day-to-day experiences
don't always reveal so much appreciation. If I'm a potential hire, it has
to be encouraging to know how a potential employer feels about
people—even if I've heard it all before in my last three jobs. And if I'm
a current and potential customer, the thought that all of these
remarkable people are there to serve me must give me goose bumps.

Behind all of the rhetoric there must be, at least, some wishful
thinking. After all, what company or organization wouldn't want to
have the very best people? And what company or organization
wouldn't want to be the best at hiring, developing, engaging, and
energizing the most talented and diverse workforce? But it simply
doesn't happen often enough. In fact, too many workers report that
their companies never really engage them or get the best out of them.
According to statistics cited in *Fast Company* magazine in 2012, the
median tenure of a U.S. worker in each job is down to 4.4 years, and
there is a growing trend toward younger workers—that is, folks in
their twenties and thirties—spending a year or less at a job.[2] Now,
these days it doesn't take a rocket scientist, a brain surgeon, or even a
hiring manager to recognize that very few people will ever again spend
their entire career with one company or organization. But having
employees stay for less than a year is a real challenge for all of us.

So if people are our most important asset, are we doing the right things to find the right employees, keep them motivated, and get the most out of them? Because unlike buildings, equipment, computers, inventory, trucks, websites, policies, procedures, and everything else that goes into creating a great enterprise, only *people* care, think, innovate, connect with the customers in compelling ways, and can go above and beyond the call of duty. But we can get them to do these things only if we think about them in very different ways, based on a clearer understanding that they are essentially strangers looking to find a home and make a real difference.

And, unlike all of the other inputs into production or service, people can leave at any moment they choose.

Let's begin this chapter by thinking about why it is so difficult to appreciate and unlock the real talent in everyone. Then we'll look at the life of an employee to see whether we need a different approach to people—an approach driven by the reality that in many ways almost all of us are strangers.

BRILLIANCE IN OUR MIDST

In 2007 Gene Weingarten, an award-winning columnist at the *Washington Post*, decided to conspire in a fascinating test of human nature.[3] He arranged for one of the world's greatest musicians, virtuoso violinist Joshua Bell, to perform during morning rush hour at one of the busiest subway stations in the nation's capital. Weingarten's idea was simple: to see how busy people would react if their daily routines were interrupted by something remarkable, and to see whether they would even realize that something remarkable was happening—though he had no intention of letting everyone in on the secret.

At the appointed hour, Bell arrived at the L'Enfant Plaza Metro station in the heart of federal government Washington, got settled into this venue, removed his violin from its case, and began to play. (If you'd like, you can even watch part of his playing on YouTube.[4]) Just another street performer standing against a wall next to a garbage can and in close proximity to a shoe shine stand and a newsstand selling lottery tickets.

In the course of forty-three minutes, Bell played six of the most revered pieces ever written for the violin—including Schubert's "Ave Maria" and Bach's "Chaconne," the latter thought by experts to be a celebration of the breadth of human possibility. In covering the event, the *Post* reported that Bell was "nondescript" looking, like many other street performers, in his jeans, long-sleeved T-shirt, and baseball cap. But it also reported that he "played like a god"—not surprising, given who he is, the surprisingly good acoustics of the station, the fact that he was playing a 1713 Stradivari purchased at a cost of over $3 million, and the nature of his playlist—these were the same violin and pieces he plays in packed concert halls around the world, where patrons regularly pay more than $100 a ticket and he regularly receives standing ovations.

But here he was, just a guy who was apparently enjoying his music and hoping to make a few dollars on a busy Friday morning. During the time that Joshua Bell played, 1,070 people walked by on their way to offices, meetings, or whatever else they are called to at the start of a workday. Of this number, 27 left money totaling $32. More interestingly, only 7 people stopped to listen for at least a minute, and only 1 person stayed to listen for more than 6 minutes. The rest hurried by—content, it seemed, to get to where they had planned to go, despite the fact that their paths had crossed with that of one of the most talented musicians on the planet.

Weingarten and the *Post* saw this experiment as a clear indication that "context" really mattered and that most people were not able to appreciate genius when it was out of place. Clearly, we don't go to work on any given morning expecting to hear great music or be surrounded by brilliance—unless we work for a leading performing arts group, in a world-class scientific laboratory, at great museum, or in some other comparable place. And most of us don't have the luxury, even if we wanted to, of getting to work late because we decided to stop and listen to a great musician. Fair enough. But we also don't go to work expecting to engage strangers in some meaningful way.

Although context does matter, we're simply not very open to new people, new music, and new possibilities. It's interesting to note that many people walked by a live Joshua Bell performance with earphones on, listening to their own recorded music. And many of the passersby probably had pressing things on their minds that made it difficult for them to let in outside music, no matter how wonderful.

Each day, in cities and towns—on the way to work, at work, at lunch, on the way home from work, or attending any number of events during the day or at the end—we pass by dozens of people who are remarkable in some way. Maybe these people aren't world-class musicians, but they are smart and compelling at something that matters, and they know things we don't know. Things that, combined with what we already know, could make us smarter, more remarkable, and more innovative and successful. Things that could literally change our lives. But we rarely find the time to lift our heads, open our eyes and ears, and connect in some meaningful way. We're just not curious and open enough to stop and listen to the music. We're too busy and focused to change our plans in order to experience new people and new possibilities.

Part of the reason is our lack of understanding of the value of strangers in our lives. If we really understood their unique promise, and its connection to our success as companies and individuals, we might be more focused in our efforts to engage them. To change this, we have to reinvent our view of people and their value.

RECOGNIZING THE GENIUS IN EVERYONE

The first question that arises is whether or not we would recognize real genius or anything remarkable if we saw it. To most people who passed him that day, Joshua Bell was just another street performer. We might have gathered that he had a reasonably high degree of formal or informal training in the violin and assumed that he was simply hoping to make a bit of money playing at a busy subway stop. After all, aren't there a lot of very talented musicians trying to make ends meet? Maybe he needed to pay his rent, or maybe he simply loved playing so much that on a free morning he would try his hand at a public performance. And if we didn't give him the time of day, we would be unlikely to realize that he was a cut above the average musician—or in his case, several cuts above.

The *Post*'s notion that we could not appreciate an exceptional performer out of context or in the press of our hectic everyday lives is important because, more often than not, the right or most remarkable people come to us out of context and almost always in the press of our hectic everyday lives. Truth be told, when we have a job or position that needs filling, we are more likely to look for the usual suspects with the "right" qualifications than folks who are compellingly different.

But what should we be looking for? Obviously, there are certain jobs that require very specialized skills—like tax accountant, Linux programmer, nuclear physicist, center midfielder for the Barcelona soccer club, marine biologist, or labor and delivery nurse. These are jobs with a required base of knowledge that you simply can't make up on the fly. But today, more than ever before, we desperately need to hire people with open mindsets and a keen gift for making the right things happen. If I had to develop a job description for practically any position, it would likely include, in addition the requisite specialized skills, most or all of the following capabilities.

Rethinking People

Business success is all about finding, developing, and engaging people who:

- Make us far better than we already are
- Ask tough questions and commit to finding and acting on the best answers

- Bring us new ideas and fresh perspectives
- Don't always agree with us
- Believe we can always be better at the things that matter
- Have a sense of curiosity and openness to the world around them and the strangers in it
- Are passionate about delivering the most compelling value to the customers we serve
- Are skilled at collaborating, sharing knowledge, and unlocking the hidden genius in everyone around them
- Can resolve our most important problems with creativity and energy
- Can discover important new business opportunities that will help us to grow

■ ■ ■

Granted, this isn't your typical job description, but we really can't afford to hire "typical" people. We already have enough people who simply did the same work at their old employer, went to the right schools, don't make waves, and think and act just like us. We need folks who are different. Sure, we know this, but we allow ourselves to get trapped into thinking that different means having a more "diverse" workforce in a very narrow sense of the word. Of course we would like to make sure that our employees and leaders reflect the world we live in and the world of the customers we serve, which means being committed to finding, developing, and motivating people of different races, ethnic backgrounds, and genders. And we know that to some degree these people will bring different experiences and perspectives that will help us see things in different ways. But most of the "diverse" people companies end up hiring are a heck of a lot like the "not diverse" folks they already have—except for their gender or skin color.

What we should be searching for are truly diverse people who are very different—in what they've studied and the way they've been trained, the experiences and accomplishments they've had, and the way they look at the world and our business.

Not that we don't want a visually diverse employee base that also includes plenty of young people, plenty of older people, and plenty of people in the middle, but we should also have people who can't stop asking interesting questions, people who won't take "no" or "yes" for an answer; people trained as artists and people trained as engineers, left-brain and right-brain thinkers, people with no formal training at all, and even people labeled as learning challenged. We should have a good mix of introverts and extroverts, and plenty of people who have no idea whether they are introverted or extroverted. And we should want all of these people, along with their uniqueness, to share a few very common traits, such as curiosity, an openness to new ideas and possibilities, a willingness to collaborate and share knowledge, and a strong desire to make us better—as identified and discussed earlier when we looked at creating a more open mindset. We need truly diverse people so that they can figure out, sometimes on their own and sometimes together, new and better ways to do the things that matter most.

We can never know everything we need to know. We need the wisdom of others in order to reach our full potential. We need people who believe that brilliant ideas can come from anywhere if we are willing to look for them; people who believe that business is a quest to meet and learn from the right strangers, both inside and outside our organization; people who are open to engaging and learning from people very different from them. We need people who believe that travel near and far with open eyes is the greatest competitive weapon that smart people possess and that if we can't try to be remarkable we should go home, because if we aspire to be average, or even slightly above average, there's really no point in being here.

Yes, we need people who will come together and live by the popular playground command: *"Go big or go home!"* In other words, do whatever you're doing to the fullest degree, or don't do it at all.

Some companies have figured out how to do this, challenging or at least modifying the conventional wisdom that the best determinant of future success is past success. They look for the best or most creative thinkers, the folks who've taken on real challenges, the folks who have followed a less traditional career path, and the folks who seem to thrive in new situations that involve a lot of learning and imagining, because conventional wisdom rarely encourages us to be the best we can be. Conventional wisdom relegates us to doing more of the same. It's the classic Catch-22 that starts with whom we hire and is set in stone by how we treat them from the moment they arrive.

THE WONDER OF NEW HIRES

If people are our most important asset, why do we mess up so badly in unlocking their talents and brilliance right from the start?

The right new hires are actually filled with fresh ideas, energy, and a desire to make a real difference. But rather than viewing them this way, we tend to think of them as people who have a limited amount of time to get with the program and get their new jobs done. After all, time is money, and we would not have tried to fill an open position unless we were desperate to get a pile of work accomplished. So companies and their human resources leaders came up with the concept of employee "orientation" as the fastest way to get the new folks up to speed on what our organization believes in, why we're so great, what we actually do, and how we actually do it. Let's show these new hires *our way*—which is obviously far better than the way they did things at their old company or, for that matter, at any time in their lives before they lucked out and got a job here. Otherwise, why in the world would they have joined us?

But what if we're not better—or at least not better at all of the things that really matter? In fact, what if we are great at some things and downright mediocre at others? Then wouldn't it make more sense to have new hires *orient us*? To have them give us guidance on better ways to get things done?

Discovering Their Value at the Start

It turns out that the right new employees are an amazing resource that we rarely appreciate. They show up on day one eager to prove that we were wise to hire them. They arrive filled with different ideas and fresh perspectives based on a new and different set of work and life experiences—ideas, perspectives, and experiences that might actually make us way more efficient, effective, innovative, customer-focused, and successful if we were willing to listen. But instead of quickly welcoming them and tapping their insights, all too often we race to mold them into more of us. And our orientation is the first step in sucking the genius right out of them. It's kind of like our very own version of the classic movie *Invasion of the Body Snatchers*. In fact, I'd argue that at the time they arrive, new employees are the most innovative folks in the building, simply by virtue of their newness and having been somewhere else where things were done differently. Not that all of their earlier ways offer insight, but there's reason to believe that some of what they know—if we are open to learning it—would help us to be better.

Given this, doesn't it make sense to find out when they arrive just how we look through their eyes? We can always do a more traditional orientation later. If so, getting their ideas is a very easy thing to do. After they complete their new employee paperwork, get an ID badge, and sign a pledge of honesty and integrity in all matters—things they could do before they even arrive—we can send them off to explore our business without any preconceived notions. And all they need, in order to accomplish this, is a nice sign at the reception desk welcoming them; a quick heads-up to everyone else that they will be joining; and a $3 clipboard from the office supply store, holding several sheets of paper with one line across the top and another line down the center to form two columns. And at the top of those columns, there should be the wonderful words "BRILLIANT" and "CLUELESS."

Then we simply ask them to wander around and talk with the strangers that they, as the company's newest strangers, will be working with. This should include the folks in their new department and also the folks in any other department that interests them, including the executive office, and our CEO. We can send them off with our blessings for the next day, or two days, or a week, or two weeks, depending on the nature of their new role and the nature of our organization. They should attend meetings; hang out in the call center, the cafeteria, or any place our people congregate; get demonstrations of how our stuff works; and connect with anyone in our organization. And each time they learn something or see us doing something that they think is totally brilliant, awesome, or the coolest thing they've ever seen in business, they will write that down in the "BRILLIANT" column. And each time they learn something or see us doing something that they think is nuts or that causes them to wonder how long we have been living in a cave, they will write that down in the "CLUELESS" column. Then, when their "orientation" is done, they'll meet with our leadership team and share their ideas—good and bad.

Sound scary? Or does it sound like a much more logical way to bring new people into a world where they're not likely to stay unless we engage them as quickly as possible?

Breaking Out of Business as Usual

I must admit that many leaders and human resource professionals are likely to have a problem with this approach, because it messes with the way we've designed our businesses. They are likely to suggest that it is impossible to get new people to willingly participate in an honest and constructive way, because saying the wrong thing would be viewed as a "CLM"—a career-limiting move. But didn't we tell these people during the interview process that honesty and openness were core values here at Company X? And didn't we also tell them that we value innovation and fresh thinking? Well, now we can demonstrate these values in action and show people that we are open to praise and criticism alike, because our overriding objective is to become the best company or organization we can possibly be—and *everyone* is critical to making that happen.

In addition to helping us out, this approach sends a powerful signal to all new employees that their ideas and input really matter right from the start. It shows that we believe they have a lot more to contribute to our enterprise than simply going through all of the stuff that we have quickly put in their in-box and that this is a place where they can make a real difference even if they stay for only a year—though we hope that they will stay, grow, and make a difference for a lot longer.

RETHINKING EMPLOYEE ENGAGEMENT

One day, as we were walking our dog in the park, our son Noah, who was twelve at the time, asked me what my "most important dream" was. It was an interesting question and one that was not so easy to answer.

"I'm not really sure," I replied—quickly trying to jog my memory. "I've had a lot of very interesting dreams, but I'm not sure which one was the most important."

"You know," Noah said, "the dream that changed your life the most. The one you actually did something about . . . like dreaming about meeting Mamma, or having children, or getting a dog, or starting your own business, or making the world a better place, or something like that."

"I guess that I did dream about every one of those things," I answered with a smile. And all of a sudden I began to understand the even bigger idea he was getting at. That each of us has a special power to dream an important dream and then to be inspired to make it come to life, rather than simply letting our dreams fade with the harsh sound of the alarm clock or the pressing demands of an urgent priority.

And isn't this what our workplaces should be helping us to do? Shouldn't they be helping us figure out what our most important work and career dreams are, and how to achieve them within our company or organization's vision and objectives?

Instead, leaders often lament the difficulty of engaging employees and getting them to be fully involved and vested in the lives of our companies and organizations. But is it the employees' fault? Or have we failed to create a more powerful connection between their dreams and potential brilliance and our success?

Just as we need to rethink the way we welcome new hires, we also need to think in new ways about all of our employees and team members. Reinventing employee orientation sets a tone for involvement, but it is only the starting point in capturing their hearts and skills. There are a number of ways to make this happen, but I would like you to do it by challenging all your employees—in a very positive way—each to become both the "visionary leader" and the "entrepreneur" of their job. Give them responsibility, right from the start, for envisioning the greatest possible value that they and their role can have in supporting your success as an organization.

Setting the Stage

Of course, we have to do a few things to set the stage for their success, but they are things we should be doing anyway:

- First, we have to paint a clear and compelling picture of our vision or purpose as an organization; how we intend to achieve it (that is,

97

our strategy); and the things that really matter to us. This is our *"Go big or go home!"* moment, and it's not something we can punt on, because it provides the essential context for bringing out the best in everyone.

- Second, we have to make sure that every employee can find his or her place in this picture—or at least a starting point—and that all employees can see the value of their role in enabling us to achieve greater success.
- Third, we have to let them know that we believe in them and their ability to do remarkable things.
- Fourth, we need to challenge them to reimagine their role and how it might be filled to create greater value for the internal or external customers they serve. This means understanding the real needs and dreams of customers and colleagues in new ways. It also means helping them figure out where they can turn for guidance and insight and which strangers—inside and outside our company—can help them to raise the bar.
- Fifth, we need to help them to develop a clear and actionable plan to guide the changes they believe we should make—a plan that identifies the resources, support, learning, and collaboration that will be required and the likely return on the company's investment.
- Finally, we need to give them the tools to succeed and the encouragement and incentives to work through any challenges along the way. And we need to give them a sense that we don't expect things to always go perfectly—that failures or blips are essential to learning how to be remarkable at the end of the day.

Rethinking Motivation

Many of you have probably read Dan Pink's insightful book *Drive: The Surprising Truth About What Motivates Us.*[5] Pink writes about the three things that motivate most people to take initiative and make a difference:

Autonomy—Having choice and control over the work you do
Mastery—Being challenged to learn and get better at work that
      matters
Purpose—Being part of something bigger

He makes a compelling case for why these are the real motivators for most of us, so it seems logical that companies and organizations might use them as a simpler and more meaningful framework for employee engagement, career development, and evaluating performance. But that's not the way most businesses work. Instead, they seem preoccupied with a relatively narrow definition of incentives—the basic "carrot and stick" approach to getting the best out of people.

But what if we challenge ourselves to think differently about the very nature of incentives? This is especially important if our real objective is to inspire every one of our employees, team members, or associates to become as remarkable as possible. Most companies and organizations, however, assume that, with the exception of salespeople, all employees are roughly the same. We don't take the time to really understand people as unique individuals with the unique potential to do great things. So we have basic pay scales and vacation scales tied to the number of years of service, and certain types of bonus plans that some employees can participate in, which are tied to achieving key metrics set in their performance plans—assuming that we actually have performance plans. We have the same basic package for just about everyone, except possibly our most senior executives, who are under a different type of arrangement. This makes it simple and easy to "compensate" people. But it really has nothing to do with getting them to be remarkable, and I'd argue that this is tied directly to our inability to effectively engage and communicate with strangers when they first arrive.

So here's an alternative: Why not ask new people, and all of our people for that matter, what it would take to get them to leap tall buildings in a single bound? To be engines of fresh thinking and action, to be innovators and collaborators in those areas where we need them most? To continuously think about better ways to do the things that matter most and the things we have not even thought about doing yet? To be fully engaged and fully committed to making a real difference and helping us to become the most remarkable and successful company or organization in our industry or any industry? Why not ask them what it would take to make their most important dream or dreams come true? Then we can tell them that, although we do have a finite amount of resources available to compensate them, we have a good deal of flexibility in how we do it. We can explain that we are open to having them figure out what combination of assignments, learning, time to explore the world and test ideas, scheduling, access to smart people and mentors, time off to recharge their batteries, and so on—as well as money—will bring out their very best. All this is tied to the organization's most important dream; their role in making it happen; and a basic understanding of their desire for autonomy, mastery, and purpose.

Do the Same Shoes Really Fit?

To make this point a bit simpler, let's assume that everyone in your company or organization needs a new pair of shoes at exactly the same time. It's not the most likely scenario, but stick with me for a moment. To solve this problem, you might:

1. Take them all to the shoe store and let them each pick out their favorite pair of new shoes. And if you really want them to be happy, you might take them to their favorite shoe store.
2. Direct them to an online shoe store like Zappos, where they could pick out their own pair of new shoes in the calm and comfort of their own office.

3. Measure all of their feet, then go to the shoe store and pick out *your* favorite style of shoes and order pairs of these for everyone in the organization in their individual sizes. It is actually an interesting idea, especially if you want to think of shoes as part of your corporate "uniform." And besides, won't everyone love wearing a pair of red high-top Chuck Taylors?

4. Go to the shoe store and pick your favorite style of shoes in your size. Then buy these same shoes in your size for everyone in the organization.

There are, of course, lots more possibilities, but we'll stick with these four for now. And if we think about them for a moment, the first choice seems to make the most sense. Most people have their own preferences when it comes to things like shoes (and they certainly have their own size feet), and they would probably do best by going to the store, looking at the possibilities, and trying different shoes on until they found a style they liked and a size that provided the most comfortable fit.

The second choice might also work, depending on the nature of your workforce and whether the online store has a reasonable exchange policy, because it's hard to get a perfect fit online. Still, more and more people today are shopping online for many things, including shoes—preferring to avoid the time and hassles that they associate with going into a brick-and-mortar store.

The third choice might also work, assuming that you have great taste in shoes or that you can create excitement about the prospect of having a "corporate shoe." Although it's not the most compelling differentiator, folks might think of it as being kind of cool, and there is reason to believe that a lot of people, especially younger employees, might think that red high-top Chucks are cool—assuming they get to wear their own size.

But the fourth choice doesn't make very much sense because, even if people were willing to go along with the same style, everyone's feet are unique, and forcing them all to wear the same size shoes will mean that only a small percentage of people end up with a comfortable fit. Yet that is exactly what most of our companies and organizations do with their incentive plans and a host of other programs and initiatives designed to bring out the best in all of their people. They offer one size and assume that it will be okay for everyone—one size of incentives, one size of training, one size of work arrangements, one option for time off, and so on—as though treating everyone the same will inspire them to do uniquely different and remarkable things.

It just doesn't work that way.

Although we are all the same in many ways, we are also different in ways that are very important to our success and the success of our workplaces.

The Potential of a Promotion

While we're celebrating the power of our differences, let's give everyone a promotion. Regularly—as another way to keep them learning, growing, and engaged.

Think back to when you were in school, and each year brought a promotion of sorts: to a new grade, new teachers, a different and more challenging curriculum, new opportunities to try your skills at new subjects and concepts that might bring out the best in you. Then, at certain epic junctures in your academic career, you'd have an even bigger promotion to a new school and a new level of learning. You moved from just one teacher in your elementary school classrooms to a number of teachers and classrooms, your own locker, and the joy of racing down crowded hallways in a few lightning-fast minutes between periods in middle school or junior high; from the raging hormones of those in-between years to the big leagues of high school, where some of the kids looked gigantic and where you actually had some choice in the things you studied. In high school they even gave us different titles:

"freshmen," "sophomores," "juniors," "seniors," and then "graduates." Then on to college, the military, travel, or a first "real" job.

At most companies and organizations the road to promotion isn't quite so easy, common, shared, or perfect. Sure, some people get promoted, but they are typically the ones on the fast track (you know, the people labeled as "high potential"), or the ones who have paid their dues, or the ones who have "sucked up" to the powers that be. After all, promotion is not for everyone.

But why shouldn't it be?

Why shouldn't we regularly promote everyone to new roles and new areas of responsibility, new chances to learn and grow, new problems to solve and new opportunities to create, new situations in which they can be energized and more fully engaged, and new situations with new people who might just unlock their hidden passion and genius? Promotions like this would be accompanied by the applause, smiles, and warm embraces of family, friends, and colleagues.

We generally believe that promotion is a reward for a job well done, but what if we viewed it as an investment in a job to be done well? Maybe the granting of a prize before it is due, or the simple demonstration of our belief in what is possible, is part of the real key to unlocking the genius, innovation, collaboration, and growth in everyone, including strangers. Maybe the best way to continually stretch our organization to reach its full potential is by continually challenging all of our people to reach theirs.

STRANGERS IN THE WORKPLACE

Most of us enter the workplace as strangers, unless we were one of the founders of a brand-new company or we joined an established organization where we already had a number of friends. As strangers, we face the challenge of getting comfortable, fitting in, and, we hope, making a difference. And our organizations face the challenge of helping us to get comfortable, fit in, and, they hope, make a difference. But they also face the opportunity of quickly creating involved and committed team members. And if they understood the real power of strangers, they would be way more successful.

I remember the first day that I arrived to start a strategic planning project with a brand-new customer who was trying to figure out how to stand out in a very crowded marketplace. I was certainly a stranger there—except to the people who had interviewed and hired me. But as a consultant, I typically begin every assignment as a stranger, and one of my initial goals is to quickly understand the customer's world as I build a set of meaningful relationships. I have a real advantage because my role gives me access to almost everyone, which isn't typically the case for new employees.

While I was waiting in the reception area prior to my first set of meetings, I met a young man named Jeff who was there on his first day at a new job. After signing in, he was met by someone from human resources who gave him his employee badge and laptop and took him to his full-day new employee orientation—the first stop in what he hoped would be a long and successful career. And maybe it will be. But I recall seeing him several times in the weeks that followed—passing by his workspace or running into him in the break room, on the elevator, heading out to lunch, or sitting at the back of the large conference room during monthly all-hands meetings. Each time I asked him how things were going, and each time he gave me the same answer: "Okay, I guess, but I don't feel very connected here. Maybe it's just something that will take a while."

"Kind of strange," I thought to myself. I had found him, in our brief conversations, to be friendly and interesting, if somewhat reserved. But he had apparently been left on his own to accomplish the work he'd been hired to do—work that he might be uniquely qualified for, but that certainly did not get at the heart of who he was and his full potential to make a difference. I started wondering, a few months later, whether he and his company had missed the chance to connect in some meaningful way, and whether we allow too many of our colleagues to remain strangers in our companies and organizations—strangers because we choose to treat them that way. This may not happen in every workplace, but it does in many of them, especially in larger organizations where it's easier to get lost in the shuffle. We don't always find the time to let others know that they really matter and that we will never reach our full potential without them. It's a simple thing, but most people have a need to be noticed and appreciated no matter how long they've been here or what they do.

EVERYONE MATTERS

Two years ago I had the good fortune to be able to celebrate the Hindu festival of Holi outside the city of Faizabad in Northern India. It's something I had only read about, and the chance to participate in this celebration of spring, fertility, the harvest, and the ancient legend of Prahlad and Holika—a story of the triumph of good over evil—was not to be missed. The festival is best known for its sense of joy, its unique ability to break down the barriers that often separate people, and the tradition of throwing and spraying brightly colored paint at each other. A dazzling array of colored powder and water is directed at friends, relatives, neighbors, coworkers, acquaintances, and even total strangers and creates a wild swirl of blues, greens, yellows, oranges, pinks, reds, purples, and other hues. In the process, everyone becomes an integral part of a veritable rainbow of color: young and old; men, women, and children; rich and poor; and people of different faiths, ethnicities, and castes. It is a canvas of possibilities. The colors liberate us from other people's perceptions of who we are. They enable us to see everyone as a joyous equal—with an equal smile; an equal voice; an equal ability to express innate creativity; and an equal ability to contribute, make a difference, and matter. This is particularly powerful in a country where caste and social standing are incredibly important for a lot of people the other 364 days of the year.

This experience challenged me to imagine what it would be like to celebrate Holi in all of our companies and organizations, many of which have their own "caste" systems of rank, position, role, training, influence, longevity, bureaucracy, and politics, and often talk about the value and equality of ideas but rarely tap the genius of all their people. Within these organizations we too often struggle to innovate and grow but rarely bring our brightest and most diverse palette to bear.

A young man's struggle to be noticed and fit into a new workplace three months after a hopeful first day; a holiday from halfway around our ever-shrinking world that strikes at the heart of what it means to be human, but only for a day—these challenge us to imagine our true potential as companies and organizations. Just think of what we could achieve if we could figure out how to connect in new and more powerful ways with the strangers we live and work with—people with different skills and backgrounds, who share a desire to make a real difference if given the chance. But instead, most companies and organizations seem determined to miss the chance to bring all of their diverse talents to life. The key is to figure out how to change the equation not just on day one, or on Holi, but 365 days a year.

SIX

Collaboration

Individually, we are one drop. Together, we are an ocean.
—RYUNOSUKE SATORO

We all know that *collaboration* is important to the success of companies, organizations, and individuals because it enables us to bring more knowledge, ideas, and perspectives to the problems and opportunities we face, and it enables us to deliver even greater insight and value to those we have the privilege to serve. And we all seem to understand the simple notion that we are much better and much smarter collectively than we could ever be flying solo. As a result, most businesses have made collaboration a top priority by stressing its value, implementing systems and tools that are designed to support greater teamwork and knowledge sharing, and launching a wide range of initiatives intended to get people to work across organizational boundaries. However, it always seems a bit strange to me when employees and leaders talk about the difficulties of working across the "boundaries" inside their own organizations. Don't boundaries typically delineate the outside of things? But leave it to humans, especially humans in workplaces, to turn departments and functions into silos, territories, and nation-states.

Whatever the case, most efforts to encourage collaboration fail to realize our real potential as individuals and organizations because they don't consider how to connect and engage with strangers. That's right, strangers. Folks we either don't know at all, don't know particularly well, or view as just too weird to collaborate with. Let's be honest: it may take two to tango, but in a world filled with people we don't really know or trust, most of us can find a lot of reasons why we would rather dance alone.

In the previous chapter we talked about connecting with people as soon as they arrive, and that's a vital starting point for building a commitment to working together. But what about all the folks who are already here and could be powerful collaborators if we made such a collaboration a more compelling, energizing, and powerful part of their lives and the life of our business?

For the sake of argument, let's assume that collaboration is difficult, especially when it involves working with people who aren't like us. Let's also assume that most potential collaborators *are* weird. These are not exactly viewpoints that I share, but they provide a wonderfully simple way to think about the world around us and to explain why collaborating might seem to be overrated. Remember what we learned about human nature in Chapter Two? First, that we all hold a lot of built-in biases and stereotypes about a lot of different people, and second, that we have an amazing tendency to believe that we know most things even when we don't and to believe we are right even when we aren't. Tied to this view, particularly when we are pressed to meet a deadline or finish a project, is the idea that "if you want it done right you should simply do it yourself"—which makes it easy to see why efforts to work together and also share knowledge don't always get traction. After all, how can someone who thinks and acts differently than we do add value to the important stuff that needs to get done when the clock is ticking?

A few years ago a new neighbor from Japan moved into our neighborhood. He seemed like a perfectly reasonable fellow in all

108

respects but one. He had a practice of walking briskly through the neighborhood—backward. On seeing this, I could come to only one conclusion: this guy was weird. Absolutely peculiar. But over time, as I saw him zipping past our house with great speed, style, and determination, then accelerating up the big hill at the end of the block, my sense of his weirdness started turning into curiosity. On closer inspection he appeared to be quite happy about his somewhat unique form of exercise and appreciative of the stares and smiles he would find along the way. And he rarely turned his head to notice a parked car or adjust to an oncoming vehicle or creature. He seemed to easily sense things around him or behind him and to be in a zone where walking backward was perfectly natural. "Different strokes for different folks," I presumed. But was he on to something worth knowing?

So one day I tried to walk backward, with much less impressive results. Picking what I thought to be the least crowded time of day, I headed out to the street, more than slightly self-conscious. Then, struggling to find my stride, I found myself walking at a humorously slow pace and turning cautiously and constantly to greet each approaching sound while keeping my arms spread wide to guard against any possible collision. "This is hard work," I thought. Especially when compared to the relatively simple task of walking straight ahead so that you can see where you are going. That was a skill I must have mastered, albeit at a relatively modest level, as a small child and tweaked only slightly in the intervening years. There haven't been a lot of innovations in the world of basic forward walking during the last fifty years, unless you consider the technique of Olympic race walkers (kind of an oxymoron) or insight from the "Ministry of Silly Walks" episode of *Monty Python* in 1970, which you can still see on YouTube. But, sure enough, with a bit of practice I started to get the hang of walking backward. Certainly not on a level to rival that of a skilled practitioner, but enough to feel that I might actually survive a couple of laps around the neighborhood—during the quietest hours of the day.

With my growing confidence, I began to do a bit of research on this practice—only to discover that it is quite common in Japan and several other countries in Asia, and that it has a lot of real benefits, like burning more calories, increasing balance, strengthening peripheral vision, and improving hearing. These seemed like things that most of us could benefit from.

Who would have figured? I guess a lot of strangers in a lot of other places. I even found time, one day when our neighbor had stopped to take a break, to ask him about his practice of walking backward and learned that it helped him to feel fitter and stay more focused and centered in other aspects of his life. "That works," I thought. "Wouldn't we all like to be more fit, focused, and centered?"

This got me thinking about just how weird most people are—inside and outside our organizations. If we simply focus on their weirdness, we can keep from having to collaborate with them. But if we learn and appreciate what they know, especially the differences that we deem "weird," we might be able to tie that to a shared sense of purpose and change the equation.

WHY COLLABORATE?

In the mid-1990s Buckman Laboratories, a leading manufacturer of specialty chemicals based in Memphis, Tennessee, decided to reinvent itself—not by getting out of the specialty chemical business, but by figuring out how to deliver much greater value to its customers within the context of the chemicals it purchased and used. Part of the impetus for this change was a growing realization that specialty chemicals were becoming a commodity and, given plenty of choices for essentially the same products, customers had increasing leverage in dictating the price and terms. If they didn't become more valuable, suppliers would have to continue to sharpen their pencils and reduce their costs and the prices they could charge.

But what if a company like Buckman Labs could not only sell chemicals but also help its customers to use them more effectively? In essence, it could add more knowledge to the mix and become the most trusted partner and advisor based on a better understanding of the customer's world and a stronger commitment to organizing and sharing the right knowledge and expertise—not simply the expertise of the one customer service representative or technical expert, but the expertise of the entire company. To be one unified company in service to every single customer: now that is a compelling idea.

And that's exactly what Buckman Labs committed to doing, beginning with a tool called K'Netix, or the Buckman Knowledge Network—a computer-based system that enabled every one of the company's 1,200 employees to communicate and share their expertise in real time, while at the same time capturing their knowledge as a growing resource base. Imagine that a customer or prospect in Singapore had a question and his or her particular Buckman contact wasn't certain of the best answer. Through K'Netix, that contact could quickly scan the knowledge base and also send a message to all of his or her colleagues requesting their input, then quickly provide the best guidance to the customer. In the process, that person would demonstrate the power of collaboration and bringing together the complete knowledge set of friends and strangers tied together by the bond of working for the same company focused on the same objective. In the years that followed, Buckman Labs continued to support the success of K'Netix by enhancing employee skills in problem solving, application expertise, customer process knowledge, and relationship building, all tied to a corporate culture of collaboration.

Collaboration takes many forms. When I think about remarkable collaborators, I usually think of jazz ensembles, symphony orchestras, dance troupes, entrepreneurial firms, and award-winning teams from a wide range of sports where teamwork is essential. These are all folks whose every move is critical to the moves and the success of their colleagues; folks who must know each other so well that they can adapt to the slightest signal or even anticipate a change in action or direction; folks who know that their colleagues are there for them and won't let them down.

Several years ago, on a day trip to visit the Dead Sea, I shared a bus with eight other people who seemed to know each other very well. These four young men and four young women were all quite upbeat and engaging and had the eight most perfect bodies I had ever seen in one place. (Not that I had ever seen seven perfect bodies in one place before.) It turned out that they were members of the Mark Morris Dance Company, one of the world's leading dance ensembles, and they were performing the next evening in Tel Aviv. Now I wouldn't mention their appearance except for the fact that I was heading to a dry and salty corner of the globe renowned for its special restorative mud baths, and the thought of spending the day with these folks, or at least the four male members of the troupe, did not do wonders for my self-esteem. As it turned out, my ego did survive the experience, and upon returning home I committed to getting myself into better shape—though you're not likely to see me dancing in form-fitting apparel any time soon.

I recall them most fondly because of the insight they shared about the importance of spending time together, getting to know and understand each other better as people first and dancers second, and then taking the time to explore the cities and countries they performed in together as a way to build greater comfort and confidence with each other.

This leads us to a few simple guidelines that should be as fundamental to the culture of your company or organization and the rest of your life as they are to a world-class dancer, a backward walker, or even a community volunteer. By following these guidelines, we can make all of our organizations—particularly larger organizations—greater engines for collaborating.

- First, before we can begin to collaborate with the colleagues and strangers we work with in any meaningful way, we must commit to getting to know them better. We must seek to establish a basis for working together that is made up, in part, of the work that must be done, but we also need to find common ground as humans. We'll need an easy and comfortable way to make this happen.

- Second, we must spend more time together learning and exploring the world around us.

- Third, we need to have a shared and compelling purpose for collaborating that motivates us to work together in order to make a powerful difference in something that matters—not simply to work together to accomplish a task.

- Fourth, we must believe that working together enables us to provide much greater value in achieving our purpose.

Which begs the question: Have you ever taken the time to really get to know the people you work with?

I don't mean just your closest friends at the office (assuming you have close friends where you work), the other people who work in your department, or the people across the hall or in the next set of cubicles, but all of the other absolutely wonderful and remarkable folks in all of the other departments who may seem to exist simply to make your life miserable. Or the ones who don't even make your life miserable but are simply names and titles posted on doors. If you did try to get to know them, you might find that:

a. You actually like them.
b. They have interests and talents beyond their job descriptions.
c. You have something in common with them.
d. All of the above.

The Power of Ten Things

This question—*Have you ever taken the time to really get to know the people you work with?*—isn't on the SAT, the Myers-Briggs, or any other assessment instrument or personality profile, but it might be more important to your success than all of those tools. For the past several years I have been challenging companies and organizations around the world to think about this question and its relevance to their short- and long-term success—and then to have conversations with each other and, in the process, create "cultures of conversation" in which they ask all of their people to commit to discovering the humanity, genius, and possibilities in their coworkers and their entire organizations. They are to do this two people at a time by making a simple and powerful human connection through a simple exercise that lays the foundation for greater collaboration.

To date, over twenty thousand people in different walks of life, positions, and levels, and across companies and cultures, have been part of my experiment. All I do is ask people to pair off with someone they don't know very well or don't know at all. Then I give them a very easy assignment: have a five-minute conversation in which you can talk about anything you like *except work*. Anything else. You can talk about your hobbies and interests, your family, where you grew up, where you went to school, what you eat for breakfast, the books you like to read, or even the fact that you were raised by wolves. Anything. Except work. And, because metrics are important, during the five minutes you have to come up with a list of at least ten things the two of you have in common. Ten things about you that are shared by another person from your company or organization whom you hardly know.

What generally happens is this: after a moment of hesitation, a quiet room begins to buzz with energy and connections—all based on having a world of things in common. Things like those in the following list:

The Power of Ten Things
A simple starting point for reinventing collaboration

Our family, our birth order, and the number of children, grandchildren, and/or siblings we have . . .

114

Where we come from and the places we've lived . . .
Where we went to school and what we studied . . .
Music we listen to or instruments we play . . .
Favorite foods and whether or not we like to cook . . .
Travel and our favorite places to get away . . .
Hobbies and things we like to do in our free time . . .
Volunteering we do to make the world a better place . . .
Our favorite season or seasons of the year . . .
Our spiritual beliefs or religion and their role in our lives . . .
Our pets . . .
The sports we play or love to watch . . .
The cars we drive . . .
Things we like to read and watch on TV . . .
People we admire . . .
Our favorite movies of all time . . .
Our favorite colors . . .
Whether we are neat or messy, late or on time . . .
And any number of other areas of interest that come up when two
    people make the time to connect

■■■

This exercise is actually rather easy to do. In fact, I bet that each of us could be paired with any other person in the world and—assuming that language was not a barrier or that, if it was, we had an interpreter in the seat behind us—we would, within just a few minutes, find at least ten things we have in common. Ten things that would begin to build a bond. Ten things that would make others a lot more like us than we ever imagined. Ten reasons why we would be more inclined to collaborate with them than not. Ten things that would make almost all of our stereotypes about them and the role they play drift away. Ten things that could spark new ideas and perspectives, based on our shared interests outside of work, that could be brought to bear in our work lives and efforts to make our companies and organizations more remarkable.

This is the power of ten things.

Once you've done the exercise with one colleague, then you could do it with another, and another, until you become part of creating a culture of conversation that is a far more powerful driver of collaboration than anything else that you or your company could do. Collaboration takes place face-to-face between humans who are open to connecting and sharing the things they know.

And then, now that some of the barriers have been reduced, you continue these conversations, to include the world of work, what other people do, the things they know best, the things they would like to know more about, the things that concern them most, and the way they look at problems and opportunities. New conversations begin to identify areas in which you can work together to think in new and more collaborative ways, and also allow you to think about whom else to involve in your efforts. In a company or organization filled with strangers, commit to making everyone a real friend and colleague by wandering around and having conversations that matter.

The Magic of a Brief Encounter

Just in case you're not convinced, let me share a quick story for an added bit of context. Several years ago I found myself sitting next to an older woman on an even older train heading north into the center of Istanbul. I'd been on old trains in many places before, but this one seemed like a relic of another era—a train that time and maintenance seemed to have passed by. And as the train made its way into town on its elevated track, the door right next to me opened suddenly over a small park, then a busy street, then an open-air market, and then a lot filled with old cars, trucks, and buses. It was an interesting or should I say an arresting view from a moving and quite noisy train going about forty miles per hour. But seconds after the door opened, the woman sitting next to me reached out, gently held my arm, and said something like "*Tamam olacak merak etmeyin*," which I could only assume meant "Don't worry. This happens all the time. We'll be okay."

To this I smiled back and said, "Thank you so much!" realizing that we didn't exactly share a common language. Or did we? After all, we were both human and this was a very human moment. In fact, I had a pretty clear idea of what she was saying even though she spoke in Turkish. And I would imagine or hope that "thank you" was a commonly heard phrase even in a place where English was not widely spoken. And none of my doubts and language inadequacies prevented her from using this moment of connection to quickly strike up a conversation with a stranger from a somewhat different land.

For the next twenty minutes we had the most wonderful conversation, aided by a student in the seat behind us, who gladly acted as our translator and coconspirator in our getting to know each other. Our conversation covered the ins and outs of Istanbul, the best shop in the Spice Bazaar to buy pistachios and saffron, traffic, religion, mosques, politics, books to read, what life was like in Turkey and the United States, our favorite foods, an unusual local drink called *boza*, children, grandchildren, old and new trains, the joys of living near the water, basketball, the Internet, and why it is almost always a good idea to talk to strangers.

During those twenty minutes we must have discovered several dozen things we had in common, and I must have learned several dozen new things. The things we had in common built a quick and powerful bond, and the new things gave us both a chance to learn and grow. All of which made it somewhat sad to say goodbye as she walked me out of the train station and pointed me to the perfect place to find a street vendor selling *simit*, Turkey's amazing answer to the bagel, an awesome round bread completely covered in sesame seeds. I was left hoping that our paths might cross again on my next visit to this city of almost fifteen million people.

It struck me that if I could find so much in common with an eighty-year-old Muslim woman on a eighty-five-year-old train in the place where East meets West, then we could all find things in common with Erik in engineering, or Susan in accounting, or Dave in contracts, or Stephanie in marketing, or Helene in the records department, and that finding out what we have in common would be a much better way to build the desire to collaborate. Better than a corporate initiative, or a collaboration workspace, or a series of group meetings designed to share information across all of our departments. Not that these ideas are terrible, but they miss the point of collaborating in a world filled with strangers.

SIZE MATTERS—BUT IT DOESN'T HAVE TO

In large companies and organizations with lots of people, lots of locations, and lots of information, it's hard to sort things out. It becomes even harder if I believe that the knowledge I hold is powerful—in terms of either protecting my position, getting a promotion, or giving me leverage in getting the stuff done that I care about most. And sharing information is hard work too, because it takes time and energy to reach out to others or capture and disseminate what I know in a useable form.

If you have ever worked in a small company or organization you probably have a keen appreciation for the role that size plays in collaborating. Try to picture the scene in a workplace with only twenty employees. Although everyone has a role to play and a set of knowledge to master, employees are also more likely to know each other pretty well, unless there are a bunch of relatively new hires. They are also more likely to know something—and probably a lot—about everyone else's role and all the things that need to get done for the business to be successful, as well as the limits of the company's knowledge and capabilities. And chances are they help out or pitch in even when a particular challenge or opportunity is not their primary responsibility, especially when a challenge is urgent and important and can use any available hands and minds. At that moment they understand that having everyone on deck is vital to getting the job done and moving the business forward. And they probably believe they can count on their coworkers in their own time of need, whether it is a work-related issue or something important going on in their personal lives.

But as companies and organizations grow, this sense that we are all in it together can start to fade along with the likelihood that we know all of our coworkers. Sure, we may know many or most of them by name—especially if we took one of those special seminars on how to remember everyone's name—but we are less likely to know much about them and what they do every day. If the organization is spread across multiple locations, we're likely to know even less about the folks who aren't in our office, factory, or warehouse. And as we get even bigger, we begin to organize people into groups based on their functions or departments. Groups like operations, sales and marketing, product development, production, service delivery, program management, IT, technical support, distribution, human resources, finance, contracts, quality, customer service, and compliance. These groups have their own specific sets of knowledge, their own ways of doing things, their own unique language, and sometimes even their own unique "look." They also tend to build internal bonds so they can strengthen their position in the organization and gain or protect the resources they need to do their job.

I'm not sure how many people it is possible for us to know well. Maybe it is close to the 150 "friends" we talked about earlier. But I continue to smile when I recall one of our customers who took great pride in his special ability to know every single employee and something special about each of them in the five-hundred-person manufacturing firm he built. Whenever he would pass employees in the hall or the plant or out on the receiving dock, or walk through their departments, he would always stop to address them by name and ask a relevant question about a family member, a hobby, or their favorite sports team. That is, until the company hired roughly its four hundredth employee and his eyesight began to decline. Then he decided that everyone in the business should wear a rather large nametag with his or her first name written very prominently, along with a few fun words to describe his or her interests. Although he suggested that this was intended to build greater camaraderie as the company grew—and it certainly wasn't a bad idea—most people knew that it was done to make it easier for *him* to continue knowing everyone.

For most of us it is a real challenge to know all of our colleagues well as our companies and organizations grow and we divide them into parts. Although we need these groups and their specific approaches to getting things done, they often become just another silo and a barrier to achieving our objectives. These silos hoard people, information, and know-how that would be much more valuable if they were shared. Yet all too often when I ask leaders to describe their organization and its culture, they begin by saying, "We have too many silos or stovepipes and not enough collaboration," almost as though that were a necessary evil of growing a business and something they can't do anything about . . . except possibly hire a consultant who specializes in silo demolition. But it doesn't have to be that way.

We just need to understand how to build connections between strangers.

Now, I know you're thinking that our coworkers aren't really strangers. After all, we know who they are, and they do work in the same organization. But we don't know them well enough to be willing to collaborate on a consistent and meaningful basis. Not unless we change the equation. Although creating a culture of conversation is a great first step, there's a lot more that we can do.

CUBICLES, QUESTIONS, AND NICKNAMES

Where we sit, how we ask for help, and what we call each other also matter.

Wander around the executive suite of almost any company or organization and you'll quickly realize how "mixed up" these people are. That's probably a good thing. Not necessarily mixed up in a confused way, but mixed up by roles and responsibilities. In one office you'll likely find the CEO or the head of the business unit or agency (in government terminology). In another office you'll probably find the head of operations. In another office, the head of sales and marketing or business development. In another office, the CFO or head of finance. In another office, the CTO or head of technology. In another office, the General Counsel or senior legal officer. And in yet another office, the head of human resources, who may be called the chief human resources officer, chief people officer, or chief talent officer. All of these executives have offices in the same place, for some peculiar reason.

Could it be that they find particular value in hanging out together? Could it be that they see tremendous merit in being in close proximity to the folks who lead other functions and are responsible for other parts of the enterprise, so they can share their ideas and perspectives on the pressing challenges and opportunities that surface in the course of day-to-day business? Could it be that they all recognize the clear and compelling logic of working across organizational boundaries to get the most important things done?

If so, you'd never know it by looking at the other 99 percent of employees. The ones who are condemned to hang out with only people in their area of the business who do similar stuff, have similar training, and approach the world the same way. Oh, sure—they could get up, grab their passport or visa, and journey off to a new territory or another part of the building to find people who are different, but that doesn't happen very often. And that's a real shame, because it limits their ability to build camaraderie and share ideas and insights with people from other parts of the organization.

Who are we kidding?

If we want to build collaboration and improve our performance, we should mix people up. Don't let them sit with their like-minded department buddies. Have them sit with a cross-section of colleagues from other functions and other departments—people with other types of expertise, of different ages and at different levels of the organization, people with different lengths of service and different perspectives on the best ways to get things done. Create new "non-departments" without all of the baggage, stigma, and groupthink we simply can't afford if we're ever going to reach our full potential. Why wouldn't we have all of these different folks sit together, work together, and learn and create together? They would get to know each other; share ideas, knowledge, and perspectives; and have the opportunity to collaborate in the regular course of doing business to bring a broader set of viewpoints to the tasks at hand.

Just like the big bosses do.

In one interesting assignment, I worked with a customer to do exactly this. But we also included members of the executive team, who all divided up to hang out and work surrounded by a cross-section of employees from every corner of the organization. Everyone had the same size cubicle with the same access to more private meeting rooms when they needed to hold private meetings. It was a powerful experiment that gave leaders a great "street-level" view of the company and served to inspire the performance of employees at all levels.

Where we sit does matter.

Asking the Right Questions

In an important sense, collaboration is also about asking the right questions and engaging the right colleagues in a quest to find the best answers. Although it's clear that we benefit from building a bond with all of our colleagues, there are certain people who can provide even more help in accomplishing our most important objectives. And if we want to nurture their engagement, it may be helpful to wander back to ancient Greece to recall a lesson from a relatively clever and somewhat renowned guy named Socrates. What's particularly interesting about him is the fact that he rarely shared many of his own ideas, but he did know how to ask a pretty smart question, and that turned out to be his claim to fame—the good old Socratic approach. In other words, he had a great gift for asking very important questions that sparked equally important conversations. And those conversations, rather than quick answers, sparked a sense of collaboration in exploring ideas and possibilities.

This approach kind of gets you off the hook. It means you don't always have to have the right answer or know what's best. But that's okay, because there are times—actually a lot of times—when we don't know the best answer to the most important questions we face. And that's a good thing, and a perfect opportunity to ask a colleague (or friend or stranger) for a bit of help. In fact, it should be standard operating procedure to seek collaborators.

Now imagine this. As a next step in creating a culture of collaboration, we ask everyone in our companies and organizations to identify the key question or questions that drive what they do every day: What is it that keeps them awake at night and is essential to their success? What questions do they face that are at the heart of achieving their objectives and moving us forward as an enterprise? Then we ask them to make their questions public by writing them on the wall or a bulletin board next to their office, cubicle, or other workspace so everyone can see them, along with an invitation to provide ideas, insights, perspectives, leads, and connections—or simply start a conversation—that could help answer their individual question or questions in new and powerful ways. This would be an invitation for coworkers from across the hall or across the business to stop by, connect, and share their best thinking on the topic, even if it isn't their area of expertise, because they might have a very different view based on either the work that they do or some other aspect of their lives that they are particularly passionate and knowledgeable about. They might just stretch our thinking—if we are open to it.

And we can then return the favor.

We might even find it helpful to use a simple and engaging tool like Pinterest as a great way to allow our people and our organizations to post their questions and interests so that colleagues can "pin" their ideas and collaborate as the spirit moves them. This website and other public bulletin boards have become powerful social media platforms for collaboration that are much more comfortable and user-friendly than most corporate knowledge-sharing portals. In fact, although companies spend a great deal of time and money setting up and promoting their own knowledge management systems—only to find that very few people participate consistently—the more public world of bulletin boards built around communities of interest and expertise is thriving. In most technical areas, people seem eager to share ideas and insights with total strangers working in the same field—with the only real incentive being some recognition of their participation and the value of their contributions. This raises a few important questions. First, why are people so open to sharing knowledge outside the confines of their workplaces? And second, what lessons does this hold for improving internal corporate and organizational collaboration? The popularity of not only Pinterest, but Wikipedia, a wide range of other wikis and forums, and sites like Trip Advisor and Yelp demonstrates the desire of people to collaborate and share their knowledge with strangers. Perhaps we would be better off casting a wider net in our efforts to collaborate by asking knowledgeable outsiders to provide fast feedback in response to some of our challenges and opportunities and, in the process, strengthen our knowledge base. It might even be a great new way to source the right talent.

It's also important to realize that this notion of sharing or posting our questions doesn't have to stop with individuals. Companies and organizations can also "post" big questions that will engage employees and spark new conversations. A great example is L-3 Communications, a leading defense contractor that built its business primarily by buying other companies—especially small and mid-size firms with niche technologies spread across a wide range of areas related to the military and homeland security. In its business model, it let these roughly one hundred firms operate as somewhat independent firms as long as they met key financial and growth targets, with no particular requirements for collaboration. But, to play Socrates (or a Socrates wannabe) for a moment, what if some bigger opportunities required more than one business unit to combine technology and know-how?

Within L-3's business model and culture, this lack of formal collaboration proved to be a significant challenge—that is, until the company recognized the opportunity to become a major player in the world of UAVs or unmanned aerial (or air) vehicles. You know, those clever airplanes and drones that are flown by pilots sitting in a building at a computer screen and can deliver a variety of weapons and other payloads. From L-3's calculation there was a clear gap between the size, capability, and cost of available UAVs and what the Department of Defense needed. It was a market opportunity that the company, with its product sets, was perfectly positioned to address if its various organizations could figure out how to collaborate.

Senior leadership asked its far-flung business units whether they wanted to play a role in building a brand-new UAV from the ground up and what knowledge and capabilities they could bring to bear. It used these two big questions to bring together ideas, people, and technologies that had previously resided in twenty different businesses. And as the company began to win valuable new business, this success began to inspire a new corporate commitment to collaboration that previously had never been part of the company's DNA.

It turns out that these big questions, and our openness to having colleagues and strangers help us to answer them, are a powerful way to shape our identity as individuals, companies, and organizations because they get at the heart of what it means for us to become more remarkable and valuable. Which brings us to the notion of how we might create more meaningful, engaging, and collaborative identities for everyone in our organizations—identities that will help them bridge the gaps that limit our success.

The Value of a Name

In the children's story "Mr. Singer's Nicknames," James Krüss tells a tale about an insurance agent name Johann Jakob Singer who takes his first trip to the island of Helgoland.[1] Upon his arrival he is welcomed by "Thunder" Pastor Rasmussen—a popular local minister with a booming voice, hence his nickname—and he is informed that "everyone who lives on Helgoland has an added name, a nickname."

"How dreadful!" Mr. Singer responds, "I am sure I will not be awarded any nickname. I am an honorable man who works and does his duty."

But little does he realize that from the moment his ship comes into view the locals have been studying him carefully and coming up with all sorts of nicknames. And the fact that he is small, thin, and storklike; wears a pair of pince-nez eyeglasses and bright yellow spats; and represents the Society for the Care of Lobsterfishermen's Widows simply adds to their interest and creativity. Yet he remains convinced that he will spend an entire week among the Helgolanders without being nicknamed, and this conviction leads him to place a wager with the pastor that he will leave the island still being called simply Mr. Singer.

It's a bet he cannot win. In fact, the locals seem entirely capable of coming up with an endless supply of nicknames. Nicknames that their visitor will discover only on the last day of his trip to the island. But more important, nicknames that show their affection for the things that set Mr. Singer apart and make him uniquely valuable.

This makes one wonder why Mr. Singer dreaded receiving a nickname in the first place. And it might make all of us wonder why we don't make more of an effort to create endearing and powerful nicknames for all of our colleagues, whether they are new to our island or have been there for most of their careers—nicknames that demonstrate in a humorous way our clear understanding of the things that set them apart and make them uniquely valuable to our current and future success. Nicknames they would be proud to own and that would strengthen their connection with everyone else in the organization. Nicknames that also break down barriers and create a greater sense of energy, engagement, and collaboration, and even a bit of humor.

REIMAGINING MERGERS AND ACQUISITIONS

Mergers and acquisitions is another area of importance to many companies and organizations, and one in which our failure to appreciate strangers severely limits our success. Research indicates that about 75 percent of mergers and acquisitions never achieve their intended results. In other words, they don't provide the return on investment that their deal makers hoped for. Is it because the real numbers are never as optimistic as we planned, or is it because few of our companies and organizations understand the challenges and promise of merging with people we don't know? Although it may be some of both, my experience suggests that the big issue is the people and collaboration side of the equation.

Unfortunately, many companies have a relatively simplistic notion of the benefits of acquiring a new business, such as:

- Gaining market share or entry into new markets
- Adding new offerings with growth potential
- Generating new revenue and profits
- Adding people with specialized expertise
- Creating greater economies of scale

These are all good reasons to acquire a business, assuming that they align with our business strategy and our position and value proposition in the markets we already serve and the offerings we already provide, and assuming that we've done our homework and picked a solid firm with truly valuable assets. But most of the time companies simply add these new assets to the old mix, thinking less about people, knowledge, and culture and more about the bottom-line results. They then will either leave the people alone to generate cash under the increased burden of the cost to acquire them, or cram their folks into existing business units with little or no integration and collaboration.

Let me ask a simple question. If you found out today that your company or organization was about to be acquired, would you quickly read a copy of *The Simple Joys of Partnering* in anticipation of the big event, or would you instead study *The Life and Times of William the Conqueror, Attila the Hun, and Alaric the Goth*? If you are optimistic, you'd probably hope that your new bosses would welcome you with open arms and minds, quickly seeking to tap your brilliance and figure out how to engage you in the most important challenges and new business opportunities. You'd hope that they would eagerly try to figure out what knowledge you and your company have that is more valuable than what they already know. You might even imagine that they would seek to learn the best things about your culture and the way you do business so they could combine them with the best things they do to create an even better merged enterprise.

And why shouldn't you be overly optimistic? After all, the initial announcements of most acquisitions are usually very kind, caring, and encouraging—something like the following: "We are delighted to announce that we have today acquired Your Company, a wonderful business with great products and services and the most fabulous and talented people on the planet, who will add immeasurably to our success. We are honored to bring them into our business and to give them all of the resources and support they need to be even more remarkable than they ever could become without us. And we can't wait to learn from them and tap into all of their wonderful capabilities." If it sounds too good to be true, that's because it is. They probably bought you to prove to their board, outside investors, or Wall Street that they could continue to grow their top and bottom lines in the face of mounting competition, a slowing economy, and their own inability to expand their core business. Yes, they couldn't figure out how to grow "organically"—a popular and fascinating choice of words—so they became a bit desperate to find another path to growth—and a joyful and productive collaboration was probably one of the last things on their minds. Sure, they'd love to create amazing synergies with you and your capabilities, but it's unlikely to happen without a radically new approach to business and one that relies on reinventing their relationships with strangers—which is something they're not likely to invest in.

It's a shame, because, just like with the promise of bringing on the right new employees, bringing on the right acquisition provides an amazing opportunity for even the best company to continue to reinvent itself—quickly tapping a wealth of new ideas, new people, new energy, new ways of doing things, and the promise of new and powerful collaborations and innovations. By finding out what you and your colleagues know best; teaching you what they know best; and committing to being a better, rather than a bigger, version of the same, the acquiring company could probably get a much better return on its investment.

Several years ago I was asked to work on an important new product with a two-hundred-person communications technology firm that had just been acquired by a well-known Fortune 100 corporation. Two weeks after I arrived, an executive from the acquiring company was assigned to lead the business and charged with "maximizing the value" of their purchase. To him this meant figuring out how to make as much money as possible as quickly as possible, and although he expressed an interest in helping them to further develop their proprietary products, his heart and his incentive plan were never really in it. The thought of leveraging their unique knowledge across the broader company never gained his support.

Instead, he tried to use his customer connections to make a series of quick product sales that would demonstrate "growth" and prove his value as a numbers-driven leader—all at the expense of the people and organization that could have provided real long-term value. It was an approach that looked good enough during the first twelve months to win him a promotion to head a larger business unit. But three years later they decided to resell the business for less than 30 percent of what they paid for it.

Most companies and organizations, and even most individuals, rarely come close to reaching their full potential because they don't take collaboration seriously or they don't understand how to collaborate with the strangers down the hallway or around the world. And although we say that working together matters, we've even designed our businesses and the way we work to minimize the likelihood that we will collaborate with colleagues in meaningful ways or tap the real power of partners and total strangers who know things that could make a difference to us. But it doesn't have to be this way.

SEVEN

Customers

It is not the strongest of the species that survives, nor the most
intelligent, but the one most responsive to change.

—CHARLES DARWIN

We all know that customers are essential to the success of any business or organization. Without them we don't have a particularly good reason to exist. In order to grow and prosper we need to continually deliver greater value to our existing customers and find new sets of customers around the corner and across the globe. And if our business is new or relatively unknown, we have to rely even more on strangers and connect in a way that will inspire them to give our offerings a try. Then, assuming we've hit the mark, we need to energize them to spread the word to their colleagues, family, friends, and other strangers.

THE NEW WORLD OF CUSTOMERS

We also know that today's customers are a moving target with changing needs, changing buying preferences, and declining loyalties. The last is due in large part to a growing disconnect between customers and the folks who serve them. As a result, customers are increasingly strangers in their business interactions, having less and less of a connection with the companies they do business with as they continue to buy more products online, rely on self-help, listen to the input of other strangers, and view more and more offerings as commodities that can be acquired for the lowest price—a price that they can easily research online for products they can purchase whenever and wherever they feel inclined to.

We had better get used to these changes and act accordingly, by reinventing the ways we connect with customers and by creating a new generation of meaningful and "sticky" experiences that demonstrate our commitment and value. Otherwise we are likely to get stuck in what I now call the "Best Buy syndrome"—a spiral of gradual or rapid business decline based on a combination of changing technology, changing customer interests and desires, and the failure of once-leading companies to react to the world around them.

Remember the days when Best Buy was all the rage? It wasn't even that long ago. Large, clean, attractive, and well-organized stores filled with the biggest selection of the latest home electronics and appliances—all there in one place to be touched, watched, listened to, tested, and compared. Interested in a fifty-five-inch HDTV? At Best Buy you could experience the latest products from most of the leading manufacturers. Curious about laptop computers, digital cameras, or washers and dryers? At Best Buy you could see many of the leading makes and models side by side. Almost anything you could ever want was in one convenient place. And for a while it seemed like a perfect formula.

But then one day this business model started to lose its appeal as major online competitors entered the marketplace—in much the same way that Best Buy's innovative business model had crushed most local appliance stores and the appliance departments of big department stores. Now you could get all of the same products for less money and with greater convenience by simply shopping on your computer or even on your cell phone, and you really didn't need Best Buy any more. Worse yet, you could visit the nearest Best Buy store, compare actual products, then purchase them online. Shouldn't they have figured this out? Best Buy had won originally because of greater selection and lower prices. They were starting to lose because of *even greater* selection and *even lower* prices—and because they were allowing their customers to become strangers.

The local appliance stores that survived in the era of big box stores did so by strengthening their connection to their customers and creating special value for those who still believed that this was important. Wasn't Best Buy's challenge roughly the same? Figuring out how to strengthen their connection with customers by providing low prices and greater value than their big, less personal, and significantly less tangible online competitors? Although you may still decide to check out the latest TV or refrigerator in one of Best Buy's showrooms, that is no assurance that you'll buy it there. And knowing this, the folks at Best Buy should have worked overtime to deliver greater value, become more personal, and capitalize on their ability to make buying tangible again. But all they seem to have done was enable you to shop with them online. Instead, they should be providing greater expertise and customer education, a truly inspirational in-store experience, significantly better warranties, opportunities to become a preferred customer with access to new product tests and the latest news and insights, free design services to maximize the value of your investments, or—why not?—your own dedicated technology advisor.

The thing is, Best Buy is not alone. In countless other industries the Internet has changed the equation, and many "old school" businesses have struggled to find the right response. Companies that counted on the loyalty of their customers, even though they often took those customers for granted, suddenly found that they had a much weaker bond than they imagined. This is true even when it comes to buying something as expensive and exclusive as a $60,000 Mercedes or BMW. In a world in which customers, even relatively affluent customers, have online access to nearly complete information about the cost and value of most products and services, their loyalty to specific high-end automotive dealerships and even specific car brands has started to waver. And only the most astute dealers have figured out how to reinvent their value equation and the entire experience of being a customer.

But let's step back a bit, because there are many businesses and organizations reinventing themselves and their industries in this world. And they are doing it by becoming a lot more stranger-centric. So let's try to figure out exactly what that means so we can tip the odds in your favor.

ON THE FRONT LINE WITH STRANGERS

It's 9:30 P.M. on a busy Saturday night in the emergency room at Holy Cross Hospital in Silver Spring, Maryland. Holy Cross is a 442-bed nonprofit teaching hospital that in 2011 was recognized as one of the top hospitals in the United States for the quality of its patient care.[1] This is a very impressive accomplishment, given that many of the country's most well-known and renowned medical centers—including Johns Hopkins, just up the road in Baltimore, and the Mayo Clinic in Minnesota—did not make the list. And the Holy Cross ER is very popular because of its accessible location and the exceptional care and experience it provides to patients—most of whom are strangers.

At first glance, the waiting room here looks no different from any other busy ER in an urban hospital. Automatic doors open to a reception desk, a modest waiting area, and a corner where a team of triage specialists quickly assesses the severity of each patient's problem. And, like many other ERs, it is also a place that serves as the first and sometimes the last resort for a wide range of strangers who come together while waiting for their moment to receive care. Many have health insurance, but a significant number do not, and they come to Holy Cross with a belief that a hospital, and especially one with a religious affiliation, will be caring, skillful, and not likely to turn them away in their moment of need. The patients come from all different parts of the community and all different walks of life. But let me give a sense of a few of them to provide a bit of context before I explain what makes this place so special and how it excels in a world filled with customers it doesn't really know.

First, there's an older woman who sits quietly with her hands folded across her chest. She has been brought to the hospital by her granddaughter, age possibly nineteen or twenty, who worries about her grandmother's repeated chest pains and irregular heartbeat and will act as her advocate and interpreter during the visit (though it is clear that many of the staff are fluent in Spanish). A few seats away from her, a young mother struggles to comfort her distraught toddler, who has a high fever, a troubling cough, and what looks like a weird science project coming out of her nose. Across from her sits a middle-aged man holding his badly swollen and bloodied left hand. It's hard to tell whether he got into a fight or he came out on the wrong end of an encounter with a glass door or window, but his appearance and the fact that he is holding a somewhat complicated conversation with himself suggest that his injured hand might not be his only health challenge. And at the end of the row, a teenage boy with a big smile sits in a wheelchair, carefully guarding an ankle he believes is broken. He tells me that it is the result of a high school wrestling match in which his coach asked him to move up in weight to fight a much larger opponent. Not that he's upset. Quite the contrary; he seems glad to have helped his team, though frustrated at how the match turned out. As a side note, he is blind, unlike his opponent, and will navigate his visit here with the help of his brother along with the kindness and skill of strangers.

This is a room full of strangers being served by strangers, brought together by health needs and circumstances—living parallel lives on a day in the life of an emergency room. Some have potentially life-threatening conditions, others have less severe issues that might have waited for primary care if they had access to it and then gotten better with a few days' rest and a bowl of chicken soup, and the rest fit somewhere in the middle. But they are all here now, along with dozens more, and the team at Holy Cross seems calm and ready.

Customizing Care

At Holy Cross they have reinvented the way emergency rooms are organized, based on their best understanding of the specific needs of the patients they expect to serve. In fact, they have actually created four distinct ERs and emergency room experiences based on the specific characteristics and needs of the people they are caring for—one emergency service for seniors, one for children, one for the rest of us, and one for problems that should be handled on a fast track—like mine on the Thanksgiving when I burned my hand grabbing a 450-degree baking sheet while engaged in a stimulating and obviously distracting kitchen conversation. So the moment anyone arrives, the staff quickly connect each patient with the right service, asking only a few additional questions about basic symptoms, contact information, and religious preference.

The last question offered a chance for a bit of levity last year when I brought my father, eighty-eight years old at the time, into the ER. It turned out that he had somewhat mysteriously lost more blood than a person should and would quickly win a pass to the intensive care unit. But as we checked in, they asked me for Dad's religious preference. Noting the large cross over the check-in desk, not unexpected for a Catholic hospital, I quickly responded that he preferred "any religion that got him the quickest and best care." This brought a smile to Dad's otherwise distressed face.

"We provide the same care to everyone," the woman at the desk replied.

"I assumed that," I said with a smile, "and I've always found that to be the case. Just trying to make light of a slightly challenging situation. And the last time I checked, Dad still preferred to be Jewish."

I'd actually called the hospital on the way in to give them a heads-up and explain that Dad's color and energy level were suboptimal, so they were ready when we arrived. Within a couple of moments he was in the ER for seniors and being treated by a doctor and a nurse.

My father's five-day stay was made much better by the fact that the Holy Cross ER understood him right away, with staff at every level trained specifically to work with seniors in a physical and emotional environment that they claim is scientifically designed to reduce anxiety, confusion, and the risk of falling and to speed the delivery of care. The physical space is designed with special lighting for older eyes, softer colors, innovative noise-reducing features, floors that reduce the likelihood of missteps, an abundance of hand rails, special mattresses that reduce pressure, blanket warmers, special pillows, pillow speakers that make it easier to listen to music or the TV, more accessible bathrooms, and easier-to-read signs every-where. There is also a thoughtful balance between the desire for privacy (and private rooms) and the increased comfort of greater visibility to the nursing station and the rest of the caregiving team. They also take special care to ensure that the staff have experience with the senior population, so there are geriatric nurse practitioners, nurses and doctors trained in geriatric care, and a geriatric social worker with deep connections to the community outside the hospital. And the pediatric ER follows the same approach, based on the unique needs of children and their families.

Being Stranger-Centric

What makes the formula at Holy Cross so powerful is the hospital's commitment to doing what is best for all of the strangers who will enter its ER. And it provides an interesting example of the challenges and opportunities we face in almost any industry. Granted, not everyone who comes to the ER is a "stranger." If someone has been there before, the hospital will have an electronic record and history that help to inform their care during the latest visit. But it's not as though people are known on a first-name or even a last-name basis. And it's not as though every returning patient is coming back for the same exact reason he or she was there before. To succeed in providing the best possible care and the best possible experience, the hospital must combine a deep understanding of the shared needs of different groups of patients with the greatest skill in quickly diagnosing and treating the specific needs of all the individual patients, or strangers, who arrive 24/7.

And that's the essential challenge for many of us, unless we work in companies and organizations that have lots of direct contact with their actual customers. We all talk about the importance of being customer-centric, but what we really mean is being *stranger-centric*. Our real task is to figure out how to create and deliver the right offerings and experiences when we might never really know the specific individuals or businesses that will buy our products, services, and solutions.

Now, I know that many companies and organizations have a very good idea of who their customers are. They hang out with them, know them by name, and may even play golf with them. They send them personalized emails, talk with them regularly on the phone, and even ask them for input on new ideas. But increasingly we don't know our customers as individuals. And that suggests the need to take a fresh look at how to connect with strangers in more meaningful ways.

UNDERSTANDING AND EMPOWERING STRANGERS

This changing reality requires us to rethink the way we *understand* and *empower* strangers. Amazon, Staples, and eBay are three companies that dominate their markets in large part because they systematically study the interests and buying patterns of the strangers they do business with and continually provide suggestions and offers for products that anticipate their needs. Each of these companies is particularly skillful at collecting and mining data as a tool in driving greater value for their customers. And, strangely enough, I actually look forward to receiving Amazon's recommendations for the latest business books and Swedish mystery novels, and I'm likely to order more toner cartridges, paper, and three-ring binders when my friends at Staples—or should I say the computer system at Staples—tells me that our office is running low. I'll still continue to spend a lot of time wandering the aisles and making purchases at my favorite brick-and-mortar bookstores, but I appreciate the somewhat scary fact that the online companies are looking out for my best interests (and their own).

Remember that a growing number of customers do actually seek to remain strangers as they search for the easiest buying experience and the lowest possible price. They'd like to get more value out of the things they buy, but on their own terms—unless we can figure out a more powerful way to engage them. That's where companies like REI, Apple, and Whole Foods Market seem to have cracked the code: by building strong bonds with strangers based on a commitment to making them smarter and more able to reach their full potential.

Not familiar with REI? It is a leading provider of outdoor recreational gear and the largest consumer cooperative in America. Based in Seattle, this unique business has been around since 1938, when a mountain climber named Lloyd Anderson and his wife, Mary, convinced twenty-one other climbers to create a co-op for high-quality outdoor equipment. Today REI sells a wide range of products for climbing, hiking, backpacking, camping, bicycling, skiing, snowshoeing, and paddling, with a clear focus on providing "knowledge and confidence to explore and discover new adventures."[2] Central to this mission is the company's history of hiring people who are informed and enthusiastic representatives for the power of outdoor sports and the potential of every member and customer to achieve ever-higher levels of outdoor involvement, ability, and joy. And their skill and interest are contagious. The company also provides a wide range of clinics, classes, and excursions, for people at all different levels, on everything from bicycle maintenance and camping skills to wilderness first aid, beginning and advanced kayaking, beginning and advanced climbing, and exploring the Galapagos, all designed to foster greater ability and engagement. Plus, REI regularly asks customers to report on experiences with new products so the company can be smarter in making recommendations—including asking me about their amazing inflatable kayak that worked like a charm for our family and friends last summer in the open water of the North Sea off the west coast of Sweden.

Connecting with Customers

So making customers and strangers more comfortable and more capable is still a brilliant formula. In fact, no matter what business you are in, it is increasingly important to make your expertise more accessible. This is an interesting departure from an older business model, in which companies used their knowledge to make customers more dependent as a way to keep their business. It's a model that continues today in many disciplines—in particular, professional services, in which people are marketed and hired because they are leading experts in their field and possess more specialized knowledge and capability than their customers or clients can ever hope to attain. This gap is their assumed competitive advantage, and businesses like law firms, accounting firms, engineering firms, and IT firms, as well as plumbers, electricians, and physicians, come to mind. For some customers this is a winning formula. "Just get it done and send me a bill." But even that is changing.

Clearly, a high level of expertise is important in many fields. After all, why would customers hire you if they could do their own legal work or architectural design, build their own ERP system, or treat their own illness? But increasingly, customers want to have a better understanding of the work that businesses and professionals do, if for no other reason than to gain greater value from the products, services, and solutions they buy.

Expanding Our Capabilities

I recall the day I switched to my first iPhone—to me, a marvel of science and technology—and I dutifully went about setting it up to meet my somewhat modest needs for connectivity and a more mobile life. I made sure the phone worked, connected my office and personal email accounts, then set up the internet connection along with a few bookmarks tied to news and sports. I even downloaded a few apps so I could read newspapers and magazines, track the stock market, book a table at a favorite restaurant, make hotel reservations and other travel arrangements, play "Words with Friends," and follow LinkedIn and Facebook. And, of course, I introduced myself to Siri—the built-in personal assistant who clearly needs her own personal assistant—and I downloaded all of my music from my iTunes library. "Wow!" I thought. "This device is awesome!"

"Not so fast, Mr. High Tech!" said Sara, our eldest daughter and resident technology expert. "Do you realize that you're using about one-millionth of this device's capabilities? It's like total overkill for you!" And she was right. This challenged me to quickly reassess my apparently pitiful digital life and then to take a bunch of classes at my local Apple store, where the folks were more than delighted to increase my knowledge and ability tenfold. Now I like to think of myself as using more than one-hundred-thousandth of the iPhone's capabilities. It's not impressive, but at least it's a start on the road to smartphone mastery. And it's tied to the understanding that more informed and enabled customers are more loyal, more likely to refer us, and more likely to spend more money. In fact, I'd argue that although

Apple's products are beautiful, brilliant, and intuitive, their greatest advantage has been their capacity to empower users to accomplish more in their mobile and digital lives—not only through classes but through the knowledge delivered by their employees, the Genius Bar, other forms of technical support, and the wealth of content and possibilities available through the iTunes store. And even though I personally use six Apple devices, I can't say that the staff there know my name.

It's not just REI and Apple that understand the value of making strangers or customers smarter. Pay close attention, and you'll see many good (and not-so-good) examples all around you. If you shop regularly or even occasionally at Whole Foods Market—the world's largest chain of natural and organic food stores—you might marvel at this company's ability to charge a premium for groceries. Granted, many of the products they offer cost more to source than products you'll find at Target, Safeway, or even Trader Joe's. And there is definitely the extra cost of distributing so much fresh, natural, and perishable stuff, even if an increasing share of it is locally grown. But Whole Foods' success is tied to getting customers to buy into a powerful ethos that connects the food they eat and the personal care products they buy to their overall health and well-being—and the company's commitment to a community of local, national, and international suppliers that are following more humane and sustainable practices. And they reinforce this connection by providing a high level of knowledge through evening and weekend classes, new product demonstrations and tastings, printed materials, and what employees share in their regular interactions with customers.

These are powerful formulas based on connecting with strangers in deeper ways to make them smarter, more successful, and more complete. And these examples suggest the need for one other change in the way we think about customers. Most businesses focus on customer needs, but remarkable businesses are all about envisioning the hopes and dreams of their customers.

But there's more to the necessity of strangers as customers than simply helping us to reach our full potential. We also need to think about the growing importance of asking strangers for their insights in making our companies and organizations more successful, and about the vital role that strangers play in making new and innovative offerings possible.

STRANGERS PROVIDE GUIDANCE

Strangers are also the fastest-growing source of insight and support in our business and personal lives. Think for a moment about the last time you took a trip that required any planning. Maybe it was a weekend getaway to a quiet bed and breakfast in the mountains or a small hotel by the beach. Maybe it was a visit to the wine country of Napa Valley or a flight to New York to go to a Broadway show or a favorite museum or to check out the new buzz of Brooklyn. Maybe you had the chance to spend a week or two in a more exotic place, like Patagonia, Morocco, or Vietnam, or to go kayaking off the coast of Scotland, Sweden, or Australia. In any event, you likely did some homework that relied on the input and insight of total strangers. Not that we don't use travel agents to advise us, or ask close friends for their guidance, but increasingly we count on people we've never met to tell us where to stay, what to do, the best places to eat and drink, and what remarkable things should not be missed.

In an earlier time that stranger could have been Rick Steves, the popular travel writer whose books and TV shows have informed countless travelers about many of the most popular and out-of-the-way places on the planet. Or you might have preferred using the *DK*, *Fodor's*, *Lonely Planet*, or *Rough Guide* series of tour books as your primary reference. Perhaps you might have relied on any number of popular travel magazines—like *Travel and Leisure*, *National Geographic Traveler*, *Budget Travel*, or *AFAR*—that offer their unique or certainly well-informed angles on the best places to travel and explore within your budget, with articles written by travel experts clued in to specific destinations of interest. And you might still choose to use these guides today. But you are also likely to go online and read the comments of other travelers—regular people who take the time to share their thoughts on the highs and lows of places they've been. Total strangers who are quick to rate their impressions and who together form a powerful new model of expertise. People you don't know at all who will help you to uncover hidden treasures and avoid places that either are too "touristy" or seem to miss the mark in serving customers.

This is part of a powerful trend toward "crowdsourcing," an idea made popular by James Surowiecki's *The Wisdom of Crowds*, which is putting strangers at the center of business today.[3] Strangers now have more power than ever before to influence both our buying decisions and the success of our companies and organizations. And we don't even have to make the effort or take the risk of engaging with them directly to gain their benefit. The Web has made it possible to share insight and allows us to decide which input is useful and which is not. It also captures the feedback of strangers in ways that can challenge businesses to be more open and transparent, and potentially more successful, as long as they are open to strangers' saying good and not-so-good things about them.

The Power of the Crowd

This phenomenon is everywhere. We buy cars based on the reviews of both experts and everyday strangers. We decide which classes to take at many colleges and universities based on professor evaluations completed by other students. We decide which movies to go to based on reviews aggregated by Rotten Tomatoes that allow us to compare the opinions of expert strangers with those of regular people strangers. We are, it turns out, increasingly indebted to strangers— assuming we value and benefit from their advice.

Some companies are even asking strangers to help them decide what products to offer. Walmart received lots of publicity when it held a competition to get new product ideas from customers. Its "Get on the Shelf" initiative generated more than four thousand suggestions ranging from the crazy to the purposeful and included a vinegar-based salad dressing that purported to cure baldness, shorts made from beach towels that dry you as you wear them, and scarves that turn into hats. Okay, so maybe strangers aren't always that clever. And no, none of these offerings made it into the company's nine thousand stores. But the winning entry, an easy-to-use repair kit for eyeglasses called SnapIt that addresses one of life's minor annoyances for the roughly 50 percent of us who wear glasses, did find its way into their stores.

But Walmart isn't alone. Another interesting example of this trend is the new business model of Popularise, a commercial real estate company based in Washington, DC, that has created an online platform for enabling local residents to recommend the products, services, and business establishments they would like to see in new buildings being developed in their neighborhoods. Simply go on their website to learn about a new project being planned or built in your community, then let them know the types of tenants that would be the right fit and that you would be most likely to do business with. It's an idea filled with real logic that runs counter to the way retail spaces are typically filled, which is to rely on demographic data and projections of "future" customers as the best determiners of market potential. Could it be that the aggregated voices of actual strangers are becoming more important and valuable than the detailed analyses and projections of experts?

Understanding the Stranger

It's not just a handful of companies that are focused on the needs and insights of strangers. In fact, companies like IKEA, the giant Swedish home furnishings store, incorporate a growing understanding of strangers into their businesses. I used to think that people either loved or hated IKEA, but now I realize that the same individuals do both . . . at the very same time. Who was the psychologist who came up with the concept of love-hate relationships? I'm not sure, but he or she was probably a conflicted IKEA customer.

People love IKEA because they offer an exciting world of home design possibilities at very affordable prices as long as you are willing to do your own assembly. And they've made this relatively easy, with products that are easy to transport and quick to assemble with the aid of a small hexagon-shaped tool and generic instructions that use only pictures. And while you are shopping they'll also keep an eye on your kids and serve you Swedish meatballs with lingonberries.

People hate IKEA because they provide uneven quality and more uneven customer service. And although they suggest that service is an important part of their business, actual experience doesn't always align. I often joke that the real reason IKEA's employees wear bright blue and yellow uniforms (aside from the fact that these are the national colors of Sweden) is so they will know with whom they are allowed to talk. *Each other*. But nobody goes to IKEA for great service anyway. Their business model is all about selling tens of billions of dollars' worth of products to strangers in lots of different countries.

No, IKEA probably doesn't care about who I am as an individual, as long as they know enough about me as part of a group or culture. And this type of knowledge has driven their success in every corner of the globe where they choose to operate. You see, the folks at IKEA have taken the time to learn a lot about how people live in different parts of the world and how they use their dwelling places. They also know the most common sizes of rooms in different countries—that is, the most common dimensions of kitchens, living rooms, bedrooms, and bathrooms. This knowledge is incorporated into the design and sizing of their furniture and room arrangements for every market they sell into. So when the catalogue or the showroom indicates that an arrangement of furniture will fit perfectly into your apartment in Shanghai, Dubai, Edmonton, Pittsburgh, or Stockholm, the odds are that it will.

STRANGERS MAKE OFFERINGS POSSIBLE

There's another, equally exciting side to the aggregating of strangers—as investors in ventures, creative projects, and social initiatives. Although most entrepreneurs, artists, and social activists have traditionally turned to family and friends for the funding needed to launch their efforts, a growing number are inviting strangers to provide start-up or seed capital through new web-based platforms located all around the globe. These websites include Crowdcube in the United Kingdom; Invesdor, based in Finland, focused on opportunities in Northern Europe; DemoHour in China; ToGather.Asia, based in Singapore; Idea.me, based in Argentina, focused on investments in Latin America; and Indiegogo and Kickstarter in the United States. Each of these sites provides a mechanism for connecting opportunities to a growing audience of strangers in a particular geographic area or around the world who are interested in supporting start-ups, innovative ideas, or causes they believe are important. There are even more specialized sites, like Gambitious, based in the Netherlands, which focuses on game design, and Apps Funder, which focuses on the development of mobile apps.

Kickstarter, which is currently the largest crowdfunding source, focuses primarily on creative projects, and has proven to be a powerful force in nurturing new ideas.[4] To give you a few examples, in March 2013 the site raised more $2 million for a new video game called *Torment: Tides of Numenera* and in the same month raised an equal amount in only twenty-four hours for a movie called *Veronica Mars*, based on an award-winning TV show that was canceled in 2007. Its biggest single campaign to date raised more than $10.5 million to launch the Pebble E-Paper Watch—a watch that can display messages from a smartphone.

Think of crowdfunding as providing a vital initial set of customers and supporters for our creative ideas, which might never have made it into the marketplace if not for our ability to connect with a world of like-minded strangers. Although our friends are important, we just don't have enough of them. And for most of us, the friends that we do have aren't rich enough to carry the day. But a world filled with interested and engaged strangers crowdfunding dramatically changes the equation and makes many more new ideas and projects possible—from documentary filmmakers in Washington, DC, to women entrepreneurs in Pakistan, and everyone in between. It's also worth noting that the rapid spread of the business of crowdfunding demonstrates the role strangers play in igniting innovation, as models that prove successful in one part of the world inspire people in another place to make something happen even when they never meet face-to-face. Or, as the website for ToGather.Asia suggests, "To Dream, To Create, Together."

Expanding Offerings

This leads us to one other important area in which strangers are fundamental to business success—because whether or not they fund our projects, strangers make a wider range of offerings possible. Think for a moment about all of the products, services, and solutions that you buy. If you and your friends were the only people or businesses buying them, they probably wouldn't exist. For new restaurants to take hold, new indie rock bands to go platinum, new travel destinations to gain attention, or new authors to make the *New York Times* bestseller list, they all need to tap the collective power of strangers. Sure, friends are important as a starting point. But strangers' telling their friends is even more important.

And it's not just the new and undiscovered who need strangers to succeed. In a world where technology and tastes are changing rapidly, even companies like Apple and Samsung are in a constant battle to capture the imaginations of strangers as they design and sell their super-cool devices. Staples needs strangers in order to keep its stores and website humming. Broadway needs strangers in order to offer new plays each season, the federal government needs them in order to support and expand our national parks, and Zipcar wouldn't be able to make cars available on an hourly basis without large numbers of strangers with a shared need. People we don't know and are unlikely ever to meet are essential to most of the offerings we value. People who might be very different from us in many ways but similar in a way that matters to a specific product, service, or solution. Without strangers, what is available to us would be way more limited. This may seem like a somewhat selfish reason for seeing value in strangers, but it is evidence of the potential for turning strangers into a powerful cohort of customers.

I'm not sure I buy into the trend for "daily deals" or coupons sent directly to my already cluttered email box. Granted, I've purchased a few offers for dinners, theater tickets, and other events from companies like Living Social and Groupon. And I know that even bigger players like Amazon are interested in this market. But I am more curious about a relatively new experiment by Living Social called 918 F Street, which brings strangers together to share unique experiences—and charges them a premium price to participate. Here, at a beautifully redesigned old building in Washington, DC, they are attracting groups of people with an interest in food, beverages, cooking, art, and ideas to connect with award-winning chefs, mixologists (a decidedly more sophisticated word for bartenders), artists, comedians, teachers, entrepreneurs, and even authors, and breaking down the barriers that separate strangers in a business world that is increasingly willing to keep them at a distance.

This idea of building a new sense of community around strangers with similar interests is nothing new. But it becomes intriguing when designed around a set of offerings that stretch our thinking about learning and the nature of social interaction. Recent programs like "Sumo + Sushi + Sake," wherein customers dine and drink while learning about sumo wrestling and watching an actual competition, and "Bourbon and Burlesque," wherein customers sample special bourbon-based drinks while learning the history and moves of burlesque dancers, show the potential for bringing strangers together to have fun, learn unusual things, and make new connections. And as strangers find value in these experiences, they tell their friends and create even greater demand. In case you're wondering, all 960 seats for the latest week of "Sumo + Sushi + Sake" sold out in a matter of days.

Reaching Around the Globe

Strangers have the potential to change the world of business, and the world at large, in even more compelling ways—addressing the needs and dreams of customers with big hopes and limited resources. One of the best examples is Khan Academy, the innovative online educational resource developed by Sal Khan that has the potential to reinvent the way learning occurs for everyone with access to a computer and the Internet. His simple idea, to provide "a free world-class education for anyone anywhere," started when he began to tutor his niece in math and science, and has evolved into a dynamic educational platform with over four thousand tutorials across a growing range of disciplines including math, science, economics, computer science, and humanities—each designed to teach basic and core knowledge, build curiosity and passion for learning, and level the global education playing field.[5] And although the original objective was to level the playing field for students in places with limited educational opportunity and quality, students in many of the world's best schools and most affluent communities have also benefited from this remarkable resource.

Other innovators, like Israeli inventor Izhar Gafni, are also creating businesses to assist strangers with important needs and modest purchasing power. Gafni's invention is a low-cost bicycle made from 95 percent recycled cardboard. It has the potential to provide an affordable means of transportation for people in the poorest villages and cities around the world. Costing only $9 to build, and likely to sell for only $20, this simple product could be a mobility game-changer for tens of millions of people.

We depend on strangers in more ways than we realize. Increasingly, they are becoming our core customers, our most trusted advisors, and the inspiration for the new products, services, and experiences we rely on. They are also becoming a powerful group of investors in making our most promising ideas a reality and inventors in imagining a world with greater opportunity. If we can't connect and get comfortable with them as an essential part of our businesses and lives, or leverage their ideas and the opportunities they present, we'll never reach our full potential.

Leadership

> If your actions inspire others to dream more, learn more,
> do more and become more, you are a leader.
>
> —JOHN QUINCY ADAMS

We all know that *leadership* is crucial to business success and that the best leaders help us to build organizations and cultures that nurture innovation, unlock the brilliance in employees at all levels, foster collaboration, and encourage new and more meaningful connections with customers. But does the leader's role need to change in a world filled with strangers and countless possibilities? To answer this question, let's begin with a simple children's story that has been around for about five hundred years.

THE PROMISE OF STRANGERS

In the French version of the classic tale *Stone Soup*, retold and illustrated in 1947 by award-winning author Marcia Brown,[1] three soldiers on their way home from the war, looking for a meal and a place to sleep, come to a modest-looking village. Upon seeing the soldiers approaching, the villagers quickly hide all of their food. It's not that they dislike strangers—though they are somewhat suspicious of them—rather, they are very poor and know that "soldiers are always hungry." The story's premise makes for an enjoyable test of wits that continues to amuse kids and their parents throughout much of the world.

As the story unfolds, the soldiers enter the village and knock on the doors of several of the homes, asking residents if they "could spare a bit of food" and "a corner where we could sleep for the night." But at each house they are told that all the food is gone and all of the beds are full. And each family appears to have a perfectly believable reason—even though the reader has already learned that they do in fact have food, which they have hidden under beds, in their cellars, and even down the well. And, truth be told, they also have ample room for a weary soldier to rest his head. So the soldiers devise a plan.

Standing in the center of the village, surrounded by many of its residents, the soldiers declare that because there is no food they will be forced to make stone soup—a rare and delicious concoction made primarily of water and stones. If this sounds oddly appealing to you, you are not alone. It is a most intriguing idea to a village full of people who have barely enough food to meet their own needs—and a short supply of new and innovative recipes. A delicious meal made from water and stones—the only two abundant resources around? It's kind of the food equivalent of renewable energy. But first they will need the largest pot in the village. The peasants quickly bring it to them. Then they will need to fill it with water and light a big fire to get the water cooking. And finally they will need "three round, smooth stones." Again the locals jump to the challenge, then gather around the pot with growing curiosity.

"Any soup needs salt and pepper," the soldiers suggest, and children quickly run off to fetch them. Then the soldiers note that although this should make a good soup, it would be even better with some carrots. Before they know it, one of the women in the village returns with her apron full.

And "a good stone soup should have cabbage," which another neighbor hurries home to find.

And "if we only had a bit of beef and a few potatoes, this soup would be good enough for a rich man's table." Now that's a request that is difficult to turn down—especially for peasants who have probably never had a rich man's meal before. Within moments, sacks of potatoes and sides of beef arrive to be stirred into the pot.

And "if we only had a little barley and a cup of milk," the soldiers continue, "this soup would be fit for the king himself." The soldiers then suggest that they actually made such a soup the last time they dined with the king! Probably not the most truthful statement, but exciting nonetheless.

At last the soup is ready, and a grand table is placed and set in the village square. A table fit for a king. And as the soup smells so good and the setting looks so grand, the villagers think that bread, cider, and a roast might make the banquet complete. And when these final touches arrive, everyone eats, and drinks, and dances "far into the night," at which time they decide that the three guests "must have the best beds in the village"—in the priest's house, the baker's house, and the mayor's house. A far cry from the reception the soldiers initially received.

The next morning the soldiers and the villagers return to the square to offer thanks and to bid each other a fond farewell, and we are left to assume that the villagers now have a new understanding of their own potential to be part of something remarkable. Potential that comes to fruition when everyone's unique contributions and abilities are brought together to achieve a bigger purpose than any one person might have achieved, or imagined, on his or her own—a delicious feast, a wonderful party, and greater openness to strangers. We are also left to wonder if the clever trio of soldiers will repeat their magic in any number of additional villages on their way home.

The retelling of this story shows what it means to lead in a world filled with strangers and hidden possibilities. I now offer six "new" rules for leaders. They shouldn't be surprising, although they are not the typical rules or principles we use when thinking about leadership. These new rules build on our earlier discussion of mindsets and the notion that openness is the real key to greater business and organizational success—openness to our own potential, where new ideas actually come from, the value of people we don't know, and the power of connecting in new and more deliberate ways.

The "New" Rules for Leaders

Essential roles for leaders in a world filled with strangers and possibilities are as follows:

1. Leaders challenge us to ask the right questions.
2. Leaders help us to see that we can always be better at the things that really matter.
3. Leaders capture our imaginations and inspire us to be remarkable.
4. Leaders empower us to discover and combine our greatest abilities.
5. Leaders encourage us to cast a wider net and to embrace the necessity of connecting with strangers and new ideas.
6. Leaders build cultures of conversation, engagement, and possibilities.

TWO ESSENTIAL QUESTIONS

As *Stone Soup* suggests, leaders provide the context for helping all of us to step out of our comfort zones and see that we can always do better, and that we have the shared ability to do something remarkable if we are open to putting our hearts, minds, and resources together. This assumes that your company or organization has an even more compelling purpose than that of the soldiers in this tale; that is, that the soup you make is all about enabling your customers to be more successful in some meaningful way. If this is not the case, then your starting point should be becoming clearer about a purpose that makes a compelling difference for those you have the privilege to serve.

You can do this by asking two essential questions:

Why do we exist as an organization?
If we didn't exist tomorrow, would it matter?

None of us can afford to be complacent in a world filled with smart customers, great competitors, powerful purposes, and a host of new and creative business models and offerings. Employees, customers, and potential collaborators all have choices, and we want to be the best choice in meeting their objectives—tied to the best possible understanding of what really matters to them. But we can do this only if we ask the right questions and, in answering them, commit to being more valuable through a unique combination of what we offer and the experience that surrounds it. And the real litmus test is whether the world, or at least your world, would be greatly diminished if you decided to close your doors tomorrow. That's why the folks at places like REI, Apple, Buckman Labs, RepairClinic, Khan Academy, Whole Foods, and even IKEA sleep well at night. They know that their offerings make a compelling difference—that they are providing their customers with greater knowledge, capability, confidence, possibilities, and results, and they happen to sell them useful stuff as part of the journey. So although your most loyal customers might be sad if you suddenly folded your tent, would they quickly find some other company or organization to fill the void? If so, you haven't been valuable enough, and you've still got some important work to do.

And that's where leaders matter most.

Let's face it: most of us will never be *that* important to all of our customers. But our leaders should ask us to try, and help us see that we can always be better and more valuable than we are today—by capturing our imaginations, and the imaginations of our customers, and inspiring us to be as remarkable as possible. Needless to say, someone else could always provide us with a comfortable and clean hotel room; or create a new web portal that helps a government agency to connect with citizens; or sell us roughly the same natural and organic food, or climbing gear, or web-based education, or exactly the same appliance parts, chemicals, or automobiles.

But try to imagine . . .

- Making travelers more comfortable, confident, and successful based on the specific purpose of their trip
- Enabling the government to deliver more timely, engaging, and impactful information based on a deeper understanding of citizen needs
- Making shoppers healthier and more knowledgeable about food, proper nutrition, and having a less stressful lifestyle
- Making climbers more passionate and skillful, and connecting them with other folks who share their interests
- Giving learners a growing base of knowledge, establishing learning cohort groups, and supporting their transition to additional education or work
- Making homeowners more self-sufficient, confident, and capable of doing an ever-increasing number of repairs and upgrades
- Enabling businesses to achieve more with the same chemicals and also undertake efforts to protect the environment
- Creating the most remarkable ownership and driving experience customers have ever had for as long as they own (or lease) their vehicle

And imagine that you could come up with the details of these ideas by combining your best knowledge with the ideas, insights, and inspirations of others from different industries and walks of life, just by being open to changing the game.

CHANGING THE GAME

In Chapter Five I talked about the notion of *"go big or go home"*—of making the choice to be remarkable as the only way to play the game. It's not enough to have a compelling sense of purpose; we also need to achieve it in a way that changes the game. So the best leaders need to challenge us to envision and create new and better business models that push beyond the bounds of what we already know.

Michael Lewis's book *Moneyball* and the subsequent movie tell the true and remarkable story of the Oakland Athletics and their general manager, Billy Beane, who were forced to compete with limited resources in the very competitive and expensive world of major league baseball.[2] In this world, teams with deep pockets—like the New York Yankees, Boston Red Sox, and Philadelphia Phillies— had a distinct advantage in their ability to pay big dollars for the very "best" players and as a result build super-teams. But the A's didn't have a lot of money to spend on players, so they had to—out of necessity, one might argue—create a different model for achieving success. Instead, they adopted the insight of a total stranger who was addicted to data, crunching numbers, and baseball statistics. His idea was to use analytics to create a roster made up of underappreciated and undervalued players who could be combined at an affordable price to build a winning team. These were players who may have excelled at only one or two things or, in some cases, nothing in particular, but whose unique abilities would, based on statistical analysis, create powerful synergies with each other.

It would take a rare (or maybe a desperate) leader to be open to an approach this different—one that flew in the face of conventional baseball wisdom, which had always relied on the ability of baseball experts to discern talent. To make a long story short, this new model proved to be a brilliant formula that continues to drive the success of the low-budget Athletics and has changed the way that many other teams, especially those in small markets, compete.

If you're not the big dog in your industry, this story will give you cause for optimism in a world that's changing quickly. And if you *are* the big dog in your industry, it should challenge you to rethink the way you do business. We can win by buying the best and most talented team members, or we can win by being scrappy and taking informed chances. And often that means placing bets on the insight of someone from outside with a very different view of our world—someone who can help us to reinvent the game we play, in an effort to be more remarkable and successful.

This need to shift paradigms is especially real in industries like government contracting, in which we know that the biggest customer—the federal government—is likely to have significantly less money to spend in the future. Clearly, if government agencies are to achieve their goals with fewer dollars, they will need partners with very different business models. Partners who can bring them new and more cost-effective ways to achieve their missions; partners who can make them smarter and more capable of doing some things for themselves; and partners willing to find ideas, solutions, and business models from strangers that will eliminate the need to reinvent the wheel. They will also need ideas from around the corner and around the world that may be found in the practices of other government agencies, other leading companies, other species, and folks driving stylish brown trucks. And the very same principle applies if your customers are consumers or private businesses. All are expecting you to better understand their world in order to help them to do more with fewer resources as you make them more complete in ways that really matter.

The Danger of "Yes"

To *go big* we will need all the energy, openness, and brainpower we can muster and a strong belief that success belongs to those who are willing and able to consistently reinvent their businesses. And our leaders will have to challenge us to never take "yes" for an answer—that is, when "yes" means making only modest or incremental changes in the way we do things, based on what we already know. Accepting that "yes" answer is, unfortunately, the way that most companies, organizations, and leaders continue to operate, but it's simply not good enough. Fearing the risk of failure, too many of our businesses stick close to their expertise and their tried-and-true approaches for getting things done. Approaches built on the sacred power of our current understanding about surviving in polar climates, renting videos in free-standing stores, making cars that won't collide, or creating new hairstyles. Approaches that act to limit how we define innovation, and influence how we hire and mold strangers into our likeness and the way we view collaboration as a mechanical rather than a human challenge—including our perception of mergers and acquisitions, and the way we take customers for granted. In essence, they dare only to be average or slightly better.

I'm consistently amused, or should I say confused, when I see the delivery trucks for a local company called Metropolitan Meat, Seafood, and Poultry. Trucks that proudly display the tag line or motto "Just a little better." I wonder if their leaders have any idea what these words convey. Is there anyone out there who wants meat, fish, or chicken that is just a little better? Or would customers like these products to be remarkable—that is, the freshest, tastiest, and healthiest that money can buy?

To get beyond saying "yes" to the same old ways, our leaders must give us permission to never be satisfied with our usual best thinking and to look beyond our walls for broader perspectives and deeper insight. They must sanction our willingness as a culture to be open to strangers and their "strange" ideas and to let us open our doors and set us free to discover new and better ways of doing things based on imagining what could be possible. If they don't, we will never reach our true potential as individuals, companies, and organizations.

Business examples that underscore the essential role of leaders in this regard abound. Consider Sony—one of the world's most remarkable electronics and technology companies—and how it failed to create a credible offering in the marketplace for digital music. This was the company that literally invented portable music with the world's first personal music player—the groundbreaking Sony Walkman. For almost twenty years, leading up to the shift to digital music players, they owned the ears of the entire world. If you had one of their amazing devices you could take your favorite music anywhere, albeit just in multiples of twelve songs found on each cassette or CD. But how many of us have Sony MP3 players today? Not very many, because Sony's leadership waited too long to enter the digital music business, and by the time they did launch a product, it relied on their own format rather than using the software that almost all digital music was already encoded in.

And then there's the sad story of Borders Books, a business near and dear to my heart. Having gone to graduate school at the University of Michigan in Ann Arbor, I had the joy of spending countless hours at the original Borders store on State Street—a place filled with soft and inviting chairs that was open until late in the night and had more new books than I'd ever seen before. It was a business model that changed the way that an entire nation experienced and purchased books. But like all business models, it would need to continually reinvent itself, and one day this remarkable company disappeared—the victim of its leadership's determination to take "yes" for an answer and to ignore the changes taking place in its industry. First they failed to see the necessity of selling books online, and then they failed to envision the growing popularity of electronic books and ebook reading devices—changes that were driven by strangers with new technologies and new business models. Borders is not alone in this. Too many of us and our leaders have an aversion to strangers and the things they know. And it is clear that the decline and sometimes complete failure of many once-great companies stem from their failure to listen to people they didn't know and, more important, didn't care to know.

There are pluses and minuses to practically every change in leadership and direction, especially when new leaders come from very different places and backgrounds. Leadership matters, and the best leaders have the keen ability to move organizations in new and, ideally, better ways. Sometimes changes involve looking internally for answers, as was the case when 3M shifted its focus to improving quality and processes. This wasn't, taken by itself, a bad idea, given a decline in the company's performance and a desire to restore the faith of Wall Street in the company's prospects for growth. But it's hard to grow by simply being more efficient; leaders must also challenge us to look outward and to engage the world—inside and outside our walls—and all of its strangers head-on. They must make those strangers a bigger factor in the way we do business. And to do this, we have to think a bit differently.

Striving for Perfection

I always start new consulting projects by challenging our customers to anticipate where the world is heading and the "perfect" solution to their challenge or opportunity—knowing that even if we could figure out how to be perfect today, we would need to rethink our notion not far into the future. And it's not that I'm convinced we will always get there, but I know that we can never win if we don't try. So I use the notion of "perfection" as a surrogate for being compellingly different in ways that really matter to customers and stakeholders as we step into the future with them—though I'm quickly told, especially in larger and more established companies and organizations, that it is simply impossible to think about perfection. There are too many obstacles along the way to being perfect that make the effort painful and pretty darn pointless. Companies tell me they don't have the talent, technology, and resources. Their people don't have the skillsets and knowledge. There are issues with engineering, and contracts, and marketing, and legal. All of which gets me more than a bit concerned.

"We're worried about the obstacles before we've even figured out how to be brilliant," I suggest, "and that's a formula for being mediocre." If we aren't willing to even be *open to trying* to be perfect or remarkable at the outset, we'll never have a chance to come close. We can always find the skills, knowledge, technology, and even resources if we are open to unlocking all of our own genius and combining it with the power of strangers. We just need to realize it.

So leaders must also challenge our organizations to be as perfect as we can be, or we will never have the chance to get to be remarkable. You can't take a train to a place worth going to without buying a ticket. But this requires leaders to take direct responsibility for making us more open to possibilities by exposing us to different people and different ways of thinking, and they can't do this if they condone old approaches and hire the usual suspects. They need to shake things up and bring in folks who aren't necessarily going to share their views of the world as employees, advisors, and stirrers of the collective pot. The charge to our leaders should be to create a place that has as its mission cultivating ideas and different perspectives—and challenging people to think in new ways. Within the fields we operate in, they should constantly be trying to cultivate new ideas and perspectives.

FOSTERING CULTURES OF CONVERSATION AND ENGAGEMENT

Even when we do something worth doing, and we are committed to doing it in a compelling way, our leaders still need to empower our people to be more open-minded, cast a wider net, collaborate in new ways, connect with people who know different things, and bring their new learning to bear in moving us forward. To do this, they need to foster cultures of conversation in which we first seek to more fully engage our colleagues and then seek to connect with the right strangers.

In Chapter Six, we explored the importance of making our big questions and challenges known first to those we work with every day. By exposing and highlighting these, we can find common ground with our colleagues, especially colleagues in other departments whom we don't know that well. This has three powerful benefits. First, it breaks down the barriers that tend to divide people in organizations and that limit our ability to share ideas in new ways. Second, it enables us to discover the areas beyond our work lives in which we have great interest, knowledge, and passion—areas that might be fertile ground for thinking in new ways. Third, it helps to develop our competency at having conversations with people we don't know well or don't know at all—a competency that makes it easier to connect with people in other places and other walks of life.

But to make this happen consistently, leaders must not only assign priority to the importance of creating a culture of conversation, but also live their business lives as though conversations with colleagues and strangers were essential to success. Imagine the power of leaders taking the time each day to connect with employees at all different levels and in different parts of their organizations—initially, to find ten things they have in common. Then imagine their ability to reconnect and learn more about each employee's role, sense of purpose, expertise, and work-related passions. Now imagine their ability to use this insight to help make powerful connections between two or more employees who might collaborate to look at pressing problems and opportunities in new ways. And that's only the start.

Next, imagine leaders making it a priority to regularly engage with people outside the business, from all walks of life, and to encourage employees to do the same: people from different industries and different occupations, people with different interests and skillsets, and people from different cultures. Leaders should be actively trying to connect themselves and their organizations with people who are remarkable in some way—whether they are entrepreneurs, world-class researchers, classically trained violinists, or homeless street vendors with a keen understanding of how to survive in challenging circumstances, who also happen to write books of poetry or play a mean saxophone. Everyone matters. And that's an idea that leaders must convey.

Now imagine leaders and other employees regularly bringing their new learning or, better yet, their new connections into the organization so that a world of important strangers can share their insights and exchange ideas—in conversations about what they know best, how they learned it, how they look at the world, and how their wisdom might help us to reframe the way we do the things that matter most. In fact, companies like Google have a knack for exposing their people to new people and new ways of thinking. One of their initiatives, which I had the privilege to participate in shortly after the publication of my last book, is called "Authors at Google." As the name implies, it brings authors from a wide range of disciplines into the company's offices to share their ideas and spark a conversation. And Google is not alone in this. A growing number of other companies and organizations are doing the same thing. In fact, another one of our customers—a highly respected science, technology, and strategy company called Noblis—has also made it a leadership priority to bring authors and other thought leaders in to broaden the thinking of their employees as they try to solve complicated customer challenges.

In a world filled with strangers and possibilities, leaders can demonstrate the importance of other points of view by becoming ambassadors for connecting people with each other and with strangers. But they will have to leave their offices and buildings regularly in order to make it a real priority—a priority that will send two powerful signals to everyone else. First, an acknowledgment that as smart as we are, we can never know enough. And second, affirmation that strangers hold a big part of the key to helping us reach our full potential as individuals, companies, and organizations. In doing this, they will also sanction the importance of looking beyond our walls, so that other leaders, and managers at all levels, will feel greater comfort getting out of their offices and connecting with new people, and greater comfort in allowing their own team members that same freedom to get out, explore, and connect with new people who could make a difference in their work.

It's really about the promise of having an open mindset.

A FEW NOTES ABOUT LEARNING

If we believe in the power of a world filled with strangers whom we might learn from, hire, collaborate with, or even invite to be customers, we must take a fresh look at learning. This includes designing and delivering programs and experiences that not only teach people to be more open, curious, and skillful at engaging others but actually connect them to strangers. We will also need to teach people a brand-new way to collaborate, based on first seeking common ground and then exploring different ideas and perspectives that can be brought together to create new and more valuable solutions. And we must reinvent the way we teach and nurture innovation. Too often, innovation training is all about learning to brainstorm and master the latest creative thinking techniques. Although these can be useful starting points for taking a fresh look at some problems and opportunities, they don't take into account the reality of where most new ideas come from: the world around us. We would be much better off taking people out into that world for focused and random exploration and discovery—where they can learn by experiencing innovation in action across all different walks of life.

We would also be much better off if we believed that in addition to being skilled learners, all of our people should be skilled teachers—sharing with each other, and with our customers, the things they know that could enhance innovation, collaboration, and success. And not just in terms of the specific roles they play and the specific expertise they have developed. We should consistently encourage people to share their knowledge and practical know-how in areas they are passionate about that might not, at first glance, have a connection to our business and the work that we do. Their interests and passions—whether they involve music, art, history, science, cars, travel, cooking, woodworking, gardening, or raising dogs or sheep—could provide a new and different window into how to improve our performance.

And we need our leaders to be equal participants in learning—not just by saying it's a good idea for everyone *else* to learn in the confines of a traditional classroom or a traditional curriculum delivered online, but by continually learning themselves and looking for opportunities to discover new information and perspectives that they feel inspired to share as the start of a meaningful conversation.

First and foremost, we should expect our leaders to lead as though anything is possible. If they inspire us to dream big; cast a wider net; and connect with a world filled with strangers and powerful new ideas, perspectives, and insights, we might rediscover our own remarkable potential to make a difference.

Possibilities

The Power of Travel

So throw off the bowlines, sail away from the safe harbor. Catch the trade winds in your sails. Explore. Dream. Discover.
—MARK TWAIN

Earlier this year, I was invited to offer a seminar on innovation for a group of general managers from some of Marriott and Ritz-Carlton's most successful hotels around the world. As part of our work, I asked them to think about a simple and, to my mind, intriguing question:

What is the real power of travel?

It's a question that goes to the heart of their business and its true value and potential, and I assumed that they would have some great ideas. After all, they are leaders in the field of hospitality, an industry based on the importance of travel, and all had, during the course of their careers, been assigned to or had chosen to work in a diverse set of places—East Asia, South Asia, Africa, Australia, the Middle East, Europe, Latin America, and North America—and hotels catering to different types of business and leisure travelers, both groups and individuals. Needless to say, their responses didn't disappoint me;

they provide a wonderful starting point for this brief closing chapter on the power of travel.

In summary, they suggested that travel enables us to:

- Discover new things and experience the joy of that discovery
- Expand our knowledge of people, places, and ideas
- Better understand and appreciate different cultures and people
- Better understand ourselves
- Experience adventure
- Build new friendships and new business relationships
- Become more worldly
- Become more fulfilled and more complete as human beings
- Gain a fresh perspective
- Take a break from or break out of the rut of our everyday lives
- Connect with our spouses, partners, and families in new ways
- Reward ourselves for our hard work and accomplishments
- Check off wishes on our "bucket list"
  and
- Grow as people

All this from simply getting up and heading out to a new neighborhood on the other side of town, or a remote village or bustling city in a country halfway around the globe.

Often, in workshops like the one with Marriott and Ritz-Carlton or in speeches to a variety of audiences, I'm asked for my one most important piece of advice, one suggestion on what our companies and leaders could do—if they could do only one thing—to spark more innovative thinking and action.

"*Travel*," I respond without hesitation.

Travel to places near and far. Travel anywhere. It's the one way to instantly gain a fresh perspective and energize your thinking about different possibilities and the reality that we can always be better at the things that matter most. This assumes, of course, that you begin with a sense of openness and with your eyes wide open to everything around you and with a belief that insight awaits around every corner—that you begin with a sense of curiosity and a willingness to discover what others know best, with real respect for the richness of their experience and how it came to be. And that you suspend judgment about everything you encounter. Nothing is better or worse. No people or culture is superior or inferior. Just different. And that difference might hold the key to your future success.

Our most popular consulting service is a program called "Team Learning Adventures," in which we take leadership teams, sales and marketing teams, customer service teams, project teams, and innovation groups exploring in some of the most remarkable cities in the United States and around the world. The goal is to unlock new ideas, perspectives, and understandings that they can combine with what they already know to solve pressing business challenges and create even greater value for their customers. It is my favorite program because in two short days it begins to teach people how to unlock their own innate potential to be explorers and innovators and, more important, to become more open-minded.

Travel, when done in the right spirit, is a powerful tool in building a more open mindset and in finding the humility we need to do great things. It also affords us the chance to be uncomfortable enough to appreciate what we have and what we know best, while it asks us to imagine that there is always a better or at least a different way to do the most important things.

And in the process, if we are open to its possibilities, it can challenge us to learn and grow in unforeseen ways, as was the case on a recent visit halfway around the world.

GETTING PAST THE FIRST BITE

If you have ever driven in the northern part of India, you know that there are more cities and towns than one can imagine along roads filled with energy, commerce, heavy traffic, cars, motorcycles, freight trucks bursting at the seams, countless railroad crossings, and lots of cows, goats, and water buffaloes. More cows than I had ever seen before, even in trips across the American plains. And, as a result, the road is also lined with the most artistic and (at times) fragrant mounds of cow dung imaginable—formed into small "towers" of what we might call drying prairie pizzas. These towers are so prevalent in practically every parcel of empty ground that they raise the question: "What the heck do you use this stuff for?" I had answered the question in my own mind by assuming that they were used as an inexpensive and decidedly renewable form of energy by people with limited resources, significant ingenuity, and a slightly different sense of smell. Though given the outside temperature during my visit in late March, I wondered if it ever got cold enough to fire these guys up. But, in fact, the real answer was a bit more interesting, because this gift from the gods—cows are gods in India—is used for cooking food. And upon learning this, I asked my host to tell me more, as curiosity quickly got the better of me.

"Local people have been using cow dung as a special way to cook their food for generations," she told me. And then she added that her cook had learned some special and delicious recipes from his mother, who lived in one of these villages and was a master of this form of cooking.

"Can we try it when we return?" I asked, excited by the opportunity to try a truly different cuisine.

"I'm sure he'd be delighted," she replied, and she called ahead to alert him to my interest.

When we arrived at her house, the cook was beginning to get the dung and food ready, and I asked if I could watch the entire process.

"I would be glad to show you," he said, placing a chair next to the spot outside where he built a fire. (Now, along with the important disclaimer that you should not try this at home without the strict supervision of a professional, let me also note that one of the great joys and even *responsibilities* of an innovation consultant is to go, when possible, wherever new experiences take you.) I must admit that as I sat there watching him light up several of the dung "briquettes" I had the particularly naïve notion that once they were hot enough he would simply place a grill over them and begin to cook the vegetables he had cleaned and the bread he had formed. But in fact, as soon as the dung became red hot, he broke it into relatively small pieces and proceeded to mix it with the potatoes, eggplant, tomatoes, and rolls so they could roast to perfection. Yes, you heard correctly. All of the food was stirred into the dung with great passion and then cooked for thirty minutes. When it was done, I watched as he removed each vegetable by hand, peeled it, and mixed it with wonderful spices and fresh chili peppers to create a mashed potato and eggplant stew and a tomato chutney that were beautiful and, dare I say, fragrant. And then he simply dusted off the rolls, sliced them into halves, and poured creamy lentils over the top.

Finally he placed everything on the table and waited for me to give it a try. As you may or may not imagine, it was delicious, and I found myself eating three helpings under the watchful eyes of the cook and the delighted smile of my host.

"It is fantastic," I said with total honesty. "It has a wonderful smoky flavor unlike anything I've ever tasted before," which was definitely an understatement. And within a moment of giving my review, I noticed a tear appear in the cook's eye.

"I am honored that you like it," he replied, "and I cannot wait to tell my mother that the visitor from America loves her cooking." Not the stranger from far away, but the visitor curious to know what others have discovered.

Now I'm not suggesting that this is likely to become my very favorite food, though this certainly ranks among my most memorable meals. And I do think that most of you reading this would have found it to be quite tasty once you got past the first bite. And isn't that what openness and innovation are all about? Getting past the first bite to seeing and then understanding what others know so well?

That is exactly the point of travel, and an essential step in our growth as individuals and organizations. But it can only happen if we believe that the world and all of the strangers beyond our walls are as vital to our growth and success as the things we already know and hold dear.

THE QUIET CAR

My guess is that many of you enjoy a bit of quiet and even solitude when traveling by train or air. And there are times that I do as well, though it is something rather difficult to achieve when traveling in coach class. Most of the time I view travel, and even the process of getting somewhere, as a great chance to connect with new people and learn new things. Other travelers can be a wonderful source of new information, inspiration, and possibilities.

Given this, it was curious that I would find myself in the "Quiet Car" for the first time in my life on a crowded train from Washington to New York—and equally curious, I guess, that I would interpret the sign hanging from the ceiling with a bit more flexibility than some of the other patrons. To me, the sign's meaning was clear: "QUIET CAR—Please refrain from loud talking or using cell phones in this car." And that seemed perfectly reasonable. I had plenty of work to do, and besides, I don't really think of myself as a loud person . . . especially not on trains. And if I couldn't spend two hours and forty-five minutes without having a desperate urge to talk on my cell phone, I should probably be in therapy.

But when two gentlemen in the row behind me struck up a conversation, albeit a not-so-loud one, I quickly learned that some people take these signs a *heck* of a lot more seriously. "This is a quiet car!" shouted a woman in the row behind them. "You're supposed to be quiet!"

This evoked the somewhat confused response that "we weren't talking very loudly."

"You were loud enough to disturb me," the woman quickly replied in a voice that was definitely loud enough to disturb (or amuse) me. And soon all was quiet, by her definition. Though that seemed to include some fellow passengers whose naturally loud breathing was even more apparent in the silence, and a gentleman right across from me who had two awesome habits: first, he seemed to pound the keys of his laptop as though performing a Mahler symphony, and second, he spent most of the trip clicking and unclicking his ballpoint pen as though it might provide some inspiration or at least relief from the problem he was working on.

And in the silence of soda cans opening, more than occasional moans and groans, newspaper pages turning, coughs, sneezes, and other unique bodily sounds, I imagined what might have happened if the sixty or so people on this train car actually decided to get to know each other. Quietly, of course. If they were to use this time to find out from each other why they were traveling, ten things they had in common, and possibly what they did for a living, what meaningful connections might arise? I even dared to imagine what new learning might take place. Perhaps they might share tips on things to see and do in the Big Apple; exchange ideas about music, restaurants, bowling, or fly fishing; share insights on hiring, teamwork, innovating, and leadership; have conversations about new business opportunities, job leads, and collaborations worth exploring; or even just talk about the weather. An unlimited set of possibilities could have been sparked if we weren't all taking the "quiet car" quite so seriously and weren't compelled to play by one particular passenger's passion for the rules.

I'm all for rules, and all for testing their limits. That's how most new ideas come to be. But maybe there are a lot of people who don't want to stretch their thinking on a Tuesday morning. They just want to keep to themselves and crunch out whatever work they have to do without the threat of somebody stirring the pot or giving them a fresh way to look at something. And there is absolutely nothing wrong with that. Maybe that's simply the way they choose to get their best work done. But maybe on that particular day I worried that much of the world and most of our companies and organizations are one big "quiet car," and I'm the one who never got the memo.

Or maybe the journey is one of the greatest opportunities for all of us to explore, connect, innovate, and grow, in order to reach our full potential.

DARING TO EXPLORE

Human history is filled with renowned travelers who have demonstrated the power of travel in opening our hearts and minds to a world of remarkable possibilities. You don't need to simply take my word for it. Two people from the Middle Ages come to mind. They traveled for different reasons but came to learn some of the same things. One was a young man from a merchant family in Venice who embarked on a journey east with his father and uncle in search of new business opportunities. Another was a young pilgrim from Tangier, Morocco, who sought to explore and understand the vast reaches of the world of his faith. Both Marco Polo and Ibn Battutah journeyed to places their contemporaries could barely imagine, and both returned years later with insights about a world filled with vast knowledge and very different people and customs.

Marco Polo left home at the age of seventeen to take a gap year that turned into more than twenty years on the road. In that time he traveled over twenty-five thousand miles through central Asia and China and ended up serving for a considerable time as a trusted advisor in the court of emperor Kublai Khan. Upon his return he wrote a book about all of the wonders he had seen, including printed books, gunpowder, paper money, spices, the compass, pasta, ice cream, and very different forms of government and organization. But most people back in Italy refused to believe that any of this was true.

Ibn Battutah left home at the age of twenty-one and during the next twenty-nine years traveled three times farther than Marco Polo did—an amazing distance of roughly seventy-five thousand miles, more than anyone would travel until the 1800s and the age of steam power. In that time he visited the north and east coasts of Africa, almost all of the Arab world, the Black and Caspian Seas, Central and South Asia, China, and most of Southeast Asia. As a devout Muslim, he was surprised by a world filled with very different customs, even among Muslims in other places, and when he finally returned he too recorded a world of enlightening experiences—experiences that many of his contemporaries also found hard to believe.

What both discovered, as have so many other travelers across the centuries, was the amazing power of travel and openness. Connecting with and learning from strangers and cultures in other places, and being open to their differences and the things we all share as human beings, can change our understanding of the world around us and of ourselves. Maya Angelou wrote: "Perhaps travel cannot prevent bigotry, but by demonstrating that all peoples cry, laugh, eat, worry, and die, it can introduce the idea that if we try and understand each other, we may even become friends."[1] We may even become better colleagues, better collaborators, more skillful innovators, and more inspiring leaders.

We win in business and in life when we use our similarities to build a stronger sense of connection and use our differences to imagine remarkable new ideas and possibilities.

That is the real power of travel and the necessity of the strangers we meet along the way.

EPILOGUE: TAKING THE FIRST STEP

Not long ago as I was exploring the "Self-Help" section of a well-known local bookstore, I noticed a young woman who seemed more than a bit perplexed. Catching my glance, she smiled and said: "I know that one of these books could change my life. I just don't know which one it is."

I wasn't sure what to say, so I smiled back, buying a bit of time to think through her predicament. I then said, with the half-baked logic of an amateur sage, "You know, we're all in that situation. Only you're smart enough to realize it." A response that seems more thoughtful in retrospect than it did at the time.

"Thanks," she replied. "I don't feel quite so foolish now."

I haven't seen her again and can only hope that she found what she was searching for. Maybe it *was* a book on one of those shelves. Or maybe it was an idea; or another person to connect with; or a story, a quote, a lesson from another culture; or a spark of inspiration from an unknown source that would give her the right direction to follow. Maybe she ended up discovering it somewhere other than the bookstore: on a journey halfway around the world or on a walk through a familiar park; during an episode of a popular TV show or a day spent at an art museum; in the words of a favorite song or the experience of a concert held in a grand orchestra hall; in a lecture on a subject she knew very little about or a familiar sign posted along a busy neighborhood street; in the mysterious ritual of someone else's religion, the best practice of a renowned corporation, or the daily life of a creature of another species.

The fact that she was looking curiously to fill a gap in what she knew—to find her own missing piece—was the essential first step. It's a step that too few of us ever take as individuals, companies, and organizations, or even as communities and nations. But it's a step that reminded me of just how close we all are to unlocking our real potential. If only we dared to be curious and open to the world around us and all of the strangers in it—in order to find something that could make the essential difference.

Each day we all pass by literally hundreds of people, places, and things that could change our lives, but we never take the time to notice them. In our rush to get from Point A to Point B, we walk past strangers who know things we've yet to discover. We walk past stores, offices, galleries, libraries, and even billboards with powerful insights to share. We observe or ignore holidays and events filled with meaning. We stroll through new or familiar places, failing to look below the surface to figure out what makes them remarkable. We watch movies, listen to the radio, read a newspaper or a blog, or search the Web without seeing the real brilliance in an idea that could matter to our life, the lives of others, or the success of our workplace or the place we call home. All because we have forgotten how to be curious and open and, lacking this skill—or rather, our confidence in this skill—are unable to believe that important ideas abound and that we can be more remarkable. But it doesn't have to be this way.

And that's the real purpose of this book. Once you understand not only the necessity of strangers, but also the power in all of us to do work and live lives that are filled with meaning, you'll become more remarkable at the things that matter most. As humans we have the amazing ability to be open and to dream, imagine, explore, learn, connect, share, collaborate, innovate, and grow, and to go big instead of going home.

So get out there and find the stranger or the idea that could change your life.

TOOLKIT

What I hear I forget, what I see I remember, what I do I know.
—CHINESE PROVERB

I developed the following toolkit to help you put the ideas in the book into practice in your work and personal lives—based on my work with customers, colleagues, and even total strangers. Think of it as a modest guide for being more open, creating new ideas that matter, tapping the real brilliance in yourself and the people you work with, building teams and partnerships that break new ground, and leading in more compelling ways. These tools can also help to change or strengthen your mindset in a way that enables you to better achieve the results you hope and dream about. Many of these tools were discussed earlier in this book, but I include some additional information here to help you feel more comfortable using them.

Here you'll find three kinds of tools:

A. Tools you can use to be more open and stretch your thinking
B. Tools you can use to collaborate more effectively
C. Tools that will help you find the perfect stranger or strangers

I've also added a few stories and a bit of narrative along the way where it seems to shed some additional light on the task at hand.

Getting out of our comfort zones requires us to take chances. Not big, scary chances, but chances nonetheless. Because thinking in new ways, exploring the world around us, and connecting with strangers does not always come easily for most grown-ups, let's begin with the remarkable story of a young man who took a chance to get you in the proper mindset for the things you'll need to do.

In *The Man Who Knew Infinity*, Robert Kanigel chronicles the short and amazing life of Srinivasa Ramanujan, one of the greatest mathematicians of the twentieth century and a person whose genius would flourish only by connecting with the right stranger.[1] In 1913, working as a modest accountant in India, Ramanujan wrote a letter to three of England's, and the world's, leading mathematical minds— H. F. Baker, a fellow of the Royal Society and former president of the London Mathematical Society; E. W. Hobson, also a fellow of the Royal Society and a chaired professor of pure mathematics at Cambridge; and G. H. Hardy, a young and rising star in the field of math, also at Cambridge. In his letter, accompanied by samples of his own work in math, he wrote of his desire to connect in order to find "help or advice" and possibly to find a place where he could learn new things and continue to develop his ideas. It was an act of hope and desperation. Although there were certainly some very smart mathematicians in his home of Madras and other parts of India, his unique gift for math exceeded their capabilities, and he longed to find a mentor who could push his thinking in new directions. This required him to reach out and take a chance—no doubt fearing the prospect of rejection.

As it turned out, both Baker and Hobson politely said "no." But Hardy, sensing a rare talent, not only said "yes" but used his growing stature to bring Ramanujan to Cambridge, where they would spend the next six years collaborating on some of the finest math ever developed—work that would prove this modest clerk to be one of the greatest mathematical geniuses of modern times. In fact, many of his formulations are being used today, almost one hundred years after his death at the age of only thirty-two, as the basis for breakthroughs in a wide range of fields. All because Ramanujan committed to reaching out and connecting.

And we can connect too, whether out of desperation—which is sometimes a powerful motivator—or out of our desire to simply find the missing piece or pieces that can take our work to the next level. And I would wager that we can even have fun doing it.

A. TOOLS TO STRETCH YOUR THINKING

What's in Your In-Box?

For many years I had the slightly odd habit of asking customers what was in their in-boxes. This was back in the days when people actually had real wooden or metal in-boxes filled with letters, memos, magazines, newsletters, invitations, announcements, and all kinds of other physical mail. And some customers would actually hand the box to me and say: "This sounds a little odd, but go ahead and take a look." I wasn't interested in their confidential corporate documents or any communications they would consider personal, but rather in finding out what things they received and read, and what meetings and seminars they attended that would keep them up to speed and engaged with the world around them. What I discovered was slightly pathetic, though not totally surprising.

It turned out that most people read stuff about their areas of expertise and their industry, along with a few general-interest business, government, or nonprofit journals, depending on the sector they worked in. Not much of a shocker there. And they also typically received invitations to trainings and conferences that fit the same profile. Events that would enable them to enhance their existing knowledge and skillsets and interact with folks just like them. This is fine if you have no interest in thinking differently, connecting with different people, and making different things happen, but you shouldn't be fine with that. No, you should be determined to shake things up, and it all starts with your in-box, even if it is now primarily electronic. You've got to make it sing with new ideas, possibilities, and opportunities to connect with the right strangers.

So the first thing you need to do is "upscale" what you read. You can easily do this on your own or as a company-wide initiative. And the next thing I suggest is that at least once a year you attend a conference that, on the face of it, has nothing to do with your work or the challenge or opportunity you are trying to address. Just pick a topic that interests you and that makes you curious to learn more. Show up with no particular agenda other than the desire to learn and think about something new, and meet some new and different people. In the process you are likely to make different and powerful connections that can help you to be more remarkable with the things on your plate.

Create a Mobile Corporate Library

Another simple and not very expensive way to stretch your thinking is by creating a small corporate library or roving newsstand filled with magazines, newsletters, blogs, articles, and even a few books from a wide range of disciplines that will get you and your colleagues thinking in new ways and about new stuff. All of these works should be focused on a world of ideas and approaches that can be applied to innovating, hiring and engaging team members, collaborating, leading, growing, and succeeding in business. The only constraint, if you can call it that, is to cast a wide net by including resources from very different disciplines, industries, and walks of life. I prefer the idea of having these resources on rolling carts, because I'd like it to be an enticing event when they pass your office or cube, and I'd like you and your colleagues to feel some pressure to pick something up and read it. Then I'd like you and your colleagues to make a commitment to sharing something you've read at each team meeting, something that has caused you to start thinking differently about a topic, challenge, or opportunity that really matters.

Stock your library with whatever things strike your fancy, but if you would like some ideas to get started, at the end of this book you'll find a list of additional resources, including some of our favorite publications at VENTURE WORKS Inc.

You can also take this idea to scale by creating a company-wide book club and picking something thought-provoking for your entire company or organization to read together and talk about. Depending on your collective bandwidth or energy, it can be a short article or an entire book; the key is to pick a "stranger" whose ideas will stretch your collective thinking about your business or an important aspect of it as a conversation starter and a way to get everyone on the same page about strategy, or an element of it, a shared challenge, or a new market or business opportunity that can be better addressed with broader thinking and new perspectives.

Get Out of the Office

Even if you create a roving corporate library or book club, it still doesn't absolve you and your colleagues of the need to get away from your desks and out of the building regularly, to wander out into the world around you with your eyes wide open to both specific places and unexpected possibilities. Try to figure out which other companies, organizations, institutions, and places in your community are remarkable in some way and commit to visiting them, at least once a month, to get you started. I can guarantee that this experience is truly habit-forming. It's surprising to me that more people don't do this regularly just to keep themselves fresh and energized. So figure out who is brilliant, cool, hip, or whatever characteristic you're aiming for and experience them firsthand in order to figure out what they know that could be adapted to your world with brilliant results. It might be another company, an award-winning nonprofit, a great local museum, a local performer or group, a trendy neighborhood, or the latest amazing restaurant. It can even be a meeting or lecture in a field you know very little about. Just get out there and open your mind to the possibilities.

You can start to do this even if you have only one free hour. Over time you and your colleagues will find such a benefit that I won't be surprised if you make this a regular part of your routine and an essential tool in problem solving, opportunity creating, and even your ongoing strategic and operational planning.

Then, along the way to wherever you decide to go, make sure to take the time to pay some attention to the unexpected people, places, and ideas that cross your path and make you pause and think.

Carry a Journal

There is a real value to always carrying a small journal or notebook with you as a way to record your observations, questions, ideas, and interactions with strangers. You can use it to jot down notes, sketch a picture or a concept, or draw a quick "mind map" of something you discover or that pops into your brain. Inspiration can come to you at the most unexpected times—so you need to be ready. Too often we get a spark of genius, then lose it in the press of our day-to-day responsibilities. So don't let your train of thought pull out of the station without capturing it.

Having a journal worked for Da Vinci, Darwin, Beethoven, Mark Twain, George Washington, author Beatrix Potter, General Patton, poet John Keats, mathematician Pierre de Fermat, film director George Lucas, choreographer Twyla Tharp, and centuries of other remarkable note takers and "doodlers," and it can certainly work for you. Over time your journal, and eventually journals, will become an indispensable resource in your efforts to think more openly and create greater value.

Spin the Globe

We can literally spin the globe and find places, people, and ideas of interest that will give us a fresh take on whatever we happen to be working on. Simply pick a place and challenge yourself to learn what they know that might be useful to you in your world and area of responsibilities. What discoveries have they made? What are the leading businesses and organizations there? What are the latest trends? What aspects of their culture might have broader appeal? What market opportunities might they provide? In what ways might they be great collaborators? Other cultures and civilizations have often changed the conversation and raised the bar in our under-standing of the world around us and our possibilities as humans, and a brief journey to another place, even if it is online or in a library, is a powerful and enjoyable place to start.

Take the Mayan civilization as an example. It began in what is now the southern half of Mexico and the northern half of Central America in roughly 2500 B.C. and had its greatest period of growth and development between the years 250 and 900 A.D. During that time the Mayans built great cities and excelled in astronomy and mathematical systems, art and architecture—most notably the Mayan "stepped" pyramids, written language, and urban design. They even made important innovations in decentralized government and local autonomy, and were pioneers in the design of rubber-soled running shoes roughly 1,100 years before Nike and Adidas became famous brands. And there are still roughly seven million people of Mayan descent alive today, continuing many of the practices of their ancestors.

Not long ago the Mayans were in the news a lot because of their apparent prediction that the world would end on December 12, 2012. Fortunately that day came and went with no more than the usual challenges—though it is important to point out that the Mayans might not have actually been predicting the end of the earth in 2012, but rather the transition to a "new age."

But, end of the world aside, the Mayans' greatest claim to fame was their calendar, which combined a 365-day agricultural calendar with a 260-day sacred calendar. The actual 365-day Mayan calendar included eighteen 20-day months, followed by a 5-day period that was considered to be unlucky. They also realized that there were an additional .242 days in a calendar year, but apparently decided not to create "leap years." And this insight might encourage you and your colleagues to realize that there are different ways to look at time. In other words, think about the role that time plays in your business or industry. Could you somehow speed up or change the clock to create unique and greater value for your customers? Might you imagine a "lucky" period in the year when you provide special opportunities for customers or employees? These are simply a couple of possibilities sparked by thinking about strangers and a great civilization that most of us know very little about.

B. TOOLS TO COLLABORATE MORE EFFECTIVELY

The Power of Ten Things Revisited

In Chapter Six we looked at a simple tool for breaking down the barriers that divide people, which I call "The Power of Ten Things." It is an easy way to create more meaningful connections between colleagues or any other people who might be interested in the possibility of collaborating to solve an important challenge or create a new business opportunity. It starts with a five-minute conversation in which we seek to discover at least ten things we have in common with another human being—ten things that have absolutely nothing to do with work. It's easy, energizing, and powerful, and it is a great way to reinforce a culture of openness and greater collaboration. Then we can use the same approach to find common ground and shared interests and complementary skills in the world of work. Once we've created enough opportunities for people to connect with as many colleagues as possible, we can use the insight gained to bring groups of people together in any number of special interest areas that can be leveraged to support our success.

We can build on this idea and take it to scale in a number of ways. First, we can ask managers to create "cultures of conversation" within their specific units or areas of the business that will encourage team members to connect, discover their similarities and remarkable talents, and build a stronger foundation for working together effectively.

Second, we can use this tool to break down any organizational boundaries. One great way to do this is by holding a series of corporate "speed dating" events. In a typical speed dating scenario—which is itself a clever social innovation—people go from table to table holding a series of brief one-on-one conversations to see if they can make a connection that is worth following up on. In companies and organizations, the approach is the same but our goal is somewhat different. Ask people to go from table to table connecting with colleagues they don't know very well or at all, with the initial objective of finding ten things in common as the basis for building rapport. Then continue these conversations by having them share information about work-related interests, responsibilities, and the big questions you are hoping they will answer as a way to jump-start better relationships and greater understanding and collaboration.

Third, we can also use the same approach to connect with customers and with new and prospective business partners.

These conversations are all about building personal connections that are fundamental to reaching our full potential as individuals and organizations. I love "The Power of Ten Things" because it is such a positive way to demonstrate the value of connecting with others, and it's an awesome starting point for connecting with strangers inside and outside of our organizations.

Post Questions, Ideas, and Curious Doodles

Chapter Six also introduced the value of asking everyone in our companies and organizations to identify and share the key question or questions that drive what they do at work. At a minimum, this will give all of our coworkers, especially the ones who don't know us well, a better understanding of what we do and the challenges we face in maximizing the value of our role. It will also give *us* a better understanding of *their* roles. This is great stuff if we are going to collaborate more effectively and provides a wonderful opportunity to share and receive input and quite possibly some new ideas and perspectives from folks who will be better able to look at our world with fresh eyes. Granted, theirs are not necessarily the eyes of outsiders with very different knowledge and backgrounds, but they are folks who aren't buried in the weeds of the things that we are often too close to. If we make a concerted effort, we can also solicit input more broadly—seeking out people we know to have different expertise and interests in order to get their thoughts.

And we don't have to just post questions. We can also post ideas that we are working on that could use some additional thinking or ideas we've discovered that are intriguing but might be more valuable in someone else's work or area. We can even start to doodle or draw a picture or a storyboard of an idea for a new offering, or a new process, or a new customer experience that we are trying to invent that might spark a moment of brilliance from a passerby or a colleague with the time to think it through. Just like the collaborative folks at Buckman Labs, who were always there for each other whenever a customer asked a question, we all have the ability to create cultures that inspire us to always be there for each other. And that's an exciting prospect.

Create a Corporate Idea Wall

We can take this very same concept and apply it to some of the big challenges our companies and organizations face as a whole by identifying one or more central places in the office in which we can create "idea walls" as a way to capture and build on our best thinking. One of our customers liked this idea so much that the leadership team decided to come up with a challenge of the month and post that challenge for all employees, in every department, to address. They chose their most popular meeting room as the place to gather input, and on the first day of each month placed a question on a big blank wall, with plenty of markers and Post-its, as well as a deadline, so people could leave their thoughts on the best ways to solve it. One month the challenge was to identify a brand-new market niche for the company's most popular service offering. Another month the challenge was to suggest ways to enhance the effectiveness of technical support. Another month they asked employees for their thoughts on how to use social media to create greater brand awareness and loyalty. And they included a note saying simply:

Please share your best thinking.
Please remember that every idea has value.

They also gave employees the option of including their names, phone numbers, and email addresses in case someone wanted to follow up, or leaving their thoughts anonymously as a possible building block for other people's thinking.

At the end of each month, the people with direct responsibility for the particular question would capture the insight their colleagues had provided as input into their work and would also try to identify suggested ideas that might have implications and value for other ongoing initiatives and future questions. The presence of this idea wall started to get a larger number of people to step out of their comfort zones in order to think about and comment on very different areas from the ones they wrestled with every day.

Create a Fun and Energizing Census

Taking a census is a great idea for companies and organizations, but it is someting that rarely occurs. Wouldn't we be more successful if we knew all of the capabilities and interests that walk into our workplaces every day? Yet most companies do a terrible job of understanding and organizing their real assets.

The key to creating a meaningful corporate census is to believe in its value and then ask the right questions. Think about the things you would like to know about all the people you work with—the ones you know pretty well and the ones who are really total strangers. What things would make you more inclined to connect with them, share and discuss ideas with them, and include them on projects and teams? You would probably benefit from knowing about their areas of expertise as professionals, but why stop with the things they do at work? They probably have a lot of other knowledge tied to their interests and hobbies, the other jobs or roles they've had in their careers, and even the social and civic activities they are involved in which would provide fertile ground for connecting in meaningful and fun ways. You would also benefit from learning about some of their special or unusual talents and experiences, as well as the types of assignments they enjoy working on.

We'll certainly learn a lot about each other through "The Power of Ten Things," but a corporate census can bring our talents and interests to a whole new level and spark an even wider range of possibilities. Think of the power of being able to know, organize, and share this information with everyone so they can see how many other folks share their expertise and interests or have unique expertise and interests that might be valuable. We can even use this information to invite people with shared or very different interests to meet-ups, brown bag discussions, communities of interest, open forums on topics of note, or presentations with outside experts on topics likely to inspire new thinking, or to launch social and recreational activities that foster greater teamwork, spirit, and engagement.

Party with the Greatest Minds in History

Not long ago I had the opportunity to meet Thomas Edison and Johannes Kepler at a science education exposition in Washington. Needless to say, it was an exceedingly lucky break. After all, Edison died in 1931 after a brilliant career as a scientist, inventor, serial entrepreneur, and astute businessperson. And Kepler lived in the late sixteenth and early seventeenth centuries in Germany, where he was one of the world's leading mathematicians, astronomers, and astrologers. So it was my great fortune to encounter both of these gentlemen at the same place, because the odds of meeting two such renowned people from different periods in history at the same time are pretty slim. But there they were, comparing notes on philosophy and the nature of the scientific process and imagining how they would be received in the current day. This suggests another interesting idea for unlocking the genius of strangers and the potential of your organization. Why not party with the greatest minds in history? After all, there is nothing stopping you.

Plan a party and invite colleagues to each pick someone remarkable from history to study and impersonate. Make sure they pick someone whose special brilliance could offer real insights into the challenges and opportunities you face as a business. Someone who devised a theory or a way of doing things that has stood the test of time or who created a breakthrough that has powerful implications. Someone who created a new industry or reinvented an old one or came up with a new way for companies to connect with their customers. Someone who knew something that could shed new light on your world today. Then use the occasion of a party filled with remarkable strangers to share ideas, expand your thinking, nurture greater collaboration, and have fun.

C. TOOLS TO FIND THE PERFECT STRANGER

Six Degrees of Kevin Bacon

In the 1990s three students at Albright College in Reading, Pennsylvania, created a party game that became an instant sensation on college campuses all across the United States. It was called "Six Degrees of Kevin Bacon," and it was based on the notion of "six degrees of separation"—that any two people on earth are no more than six personal connections away from each other. Their game posited that anyone who had ever worked in Hollywood could be connected to the actor Kevin Bacon through six or fewer connections.

In case you haven't heard of Kevin Bacon, he is a popular American actor who has appeared in a number of well-known movies, including *Animal House, Footloose, Diner, The River Wild, A Few Good Men, JFK, Apollo 13*, and *Mystic River*. And although their game was fun, its real benefit was to call greater attention to the notion that we are way more interconnected, even in our diverse world of more than seven billion people, than we might ever imagine. The idea of "six degrees of separation" or "small world theory" has been around for a while, and leading scientists have attempted to prove that a well-defined structure of social networks connects the world.[2] But a couple of years ago the British Broadcasting Corporation decided to put this idea to a test in an intriguing experiment based on another well-known experiment from the 1960s. Their idea was simple: give forty packages to random people around the world and ask them to get the packages to a scientist in Boston named Marc Vidal, using contacts they know on a first-name basis.[3] Those contacts would then have to give the packages to their contacts, and so on. In the end, three of the packages found their way to Mr. Vidal, including one that started its journey in a remote village in Kenya. And it took, on average, six contacts to get there. You can watch this experiment and learn more about the theory behind it by watching the BBC special referenced in the Notes section of the book, Chapter Four, note 1. This raises the question of how you might leverage your contacts to connect with the right strangers—people who by virtue of their backgrounds and knowledge might hold the key to a challenge you are facing. If the theory of six degrees of separation holds true, you should be able to connect with almost anyone else on the planet by taking a fresh look at whom you know and envisioning whom they might know as the starting point. So although I've suggested that the people we know aren't likely to get us where we need to go, they are often amazingly valuable in helping us to reach beyond our connections.

What if we could connect with anyone else in the world, to exchange ideas, gain unique insight, and build a working relationship or a friendship based on mutual respect? Clearly the best starting point is our ability to build and energize our own personal and professional networks, and tools like Facebook and LinkedIn give us a way to do exactly that. So although I may have roughly a thousand LinkedIn connections, not all of whom are my closest and dearest friends and colleagues, the clever folks at LinkedIn continually remind me that I am no more than two degrees of separation away from more than *fourteen million* people. People I might connect with if I had the time, energy, mindset, and inclination to ask my contacts to introduce me to their contacts.

And if I had the courage, like Srinivasa Ramanujan, I could write any one of them a letter or send an email suggesting the possibility of mutual benefit and learning.

The Power of Taking a Chance

We never know what will happen when we make the effort to connect with strangers, though I believe engaging another person, especially someone very different from us, is rarely a bad experience. That's why I go out of my way to meet new people. At worst, I learn something new about them and about myself. At best, I end up building a relationship that could last a lifetime.

Yet for many us it is very hard to take the first step. Not that we don't end up doing it in many aspects of our lives. We apply for jobs and go to job interviews with total strangers—maybe because we realize that it is unavoidable. We take classes taught by total strangers and sometimes end up building new friendships. We go to parties and other social events where we meet new people, and though it is often awkward, we survive and even connect in meaningful ways. We take trips to new places and, if we are lucky, return home with wonderful stories of experiences made more special by meeting other travelers or engaging the locals. And we even allow ourselves to go on blind dates, believing it might be the best way to meet a perfect stranger.

For four years prior to starting my own consulting firm I lived in Washington, DC and worked for a company based in Manhattan. Every Monday I would take the 6:00 A.M. train to New York City, and every Friday I would take the 6:00 P.M. train home. Though this made for long weeks away from home, it was fun and even energizing to be living in two very interesting places. But it was definitely a challenge for my social life. Many of my friends, however, were eager to be helpful—calling to arrange blind dates for me with women they knew at work or met in other aspects of their lives.

"Sure," I would say after hearing a few things about the potential partner. "I'm always open to meeting new people."

"Great," they would reply. "I'll arrange for lunch or dinner Saturday, then let you know the details."

And on the face of it, getting "fixed up" by friends seemed like a reasonable idea. After all, I'd been taught to believe that friends know us best, so their recommendations should be as close to spot-on as we could hope for. Way better than taking out a personal ad (a semi-common idea in the 1980s), going to parties, taking classes, or—God forbid—meeting someone in a bar. At that time the public Internet and online dating had yet to be invented. So I greeted each arranged meeting with a sense of curiosity and openness, imagining that one of these dates might turn into a lasting relationship. But after four years and roughly thirty blind dates, I was left with a sinking feeling that meeting the right person might not be in the cards. Sure, friends had the right intentions, and they often based their imperfect matches on things that I really liked—like my love of kids, dogs, sports, travel, theater, art, and doing volunteer work. But the barriers to making a suggestion were, when you got right down to it, low or nonexistent. "There's a new associate at our office," a typical call might begin, "and she likes hiking, and she tutors second graders. Should I arrange for the two of you to meet for dinner Saturday night?" "Why not?" I thought.

This imperfect process resulted in a total of three second dates. In each case, either the woman was looking for something different or I was looking for something different, or there just wasn't the elusive "chemistry." And I remember quite clearly, after the last blind date, calling one of my closest friends to thank him for the attempt, even though the woman in question, a very successful patent lawyer, had spent most of the evening talking about her love of dried flowers. At which point he apologized (though there was no need to) and then suggested something that would change my mindset and my life.

"You know," he said, with the enthusiasm of someone about to be released from prison, "your field is innovation. Surely you can figure out a better way to find a partner!?"

That was just the challenge I needed to jog me from my complacency and reliance on a time-tested way of doing things that didn't have a stellar track record. For the next several weeks I decided to scan the world for ideas, until the fundamental premise of every TV game show came to me: in order to win a significant prize, the contestants had to take a risk, and they often had only one chance. It was a concept I would apply to my friends and not to myself. After all, hadn't I already taken enough risks by going on all these blind dates?

The idea turned out to be remarkably simple. I would send a letter to fifteen friends with an offer they couldn't ignore:

I'll give two free round-trip plane tickets to anywhere in the world to the person who introduces me to someone I end up having a long-term relationship with.

The only catch—each friend got just one try.

And that one catch turned out to make all the difference. Friends started introducing me to women who were a lot more impressive than I was—the head of neurosurgery at a leading university medical center, a partner at a prestigious law firm, the staff director for a well-known senator. And they were all willing to go out with me. Who would have imagined? I must admit, though, that none of those three introductions led to a second date. But the fourth "contestant" proved to be a different story. She was a nurse by training and the director of women's services at a local hospital. But more important, she was the kindest, least pretentious, and most thoughtful person I had ever met. And the rest, as they say, is history.

Connecting with strangers often means taking a chance against the odds. But often there isn't a better way to accomplish the things that matter most in work, life, and even love. And giving up is not a viable option in matters of great importance. Needless to say, I'm now partial to the idea of contests for trying to meet the perfect stranger. But I'll leave you to not only try the ideas I've suggested here, but also imagine any number of ways that you might be able to reach out and connect with someone who might make a compelling difference in your work or personal life. And if holding a contest isn't your preference, you might choose to design an event or a scavenger hunt to support a local nonprofit and invite the most interesting strangers in your community to participate. Or write an article on a subject that matters and use it to open the door to remarkable people who might be inspired to share ideas with someone who never stops thinking about what is possible. Or make someone an offer he or she can't refuse. Or send an email, or a good old-fashioned letter. Or simply walk up to someone and say, "Hello."

All that matters is finding a way to connect in order to discover or rediscover the necessity of strangers.

ADDITIONAL RESOURCES

I've mentioned the power of reading new things throughout this book, and have included this resources section to help you in this effort. It's organized into two parts. The first part provides suggested reading beyond the books listed in my notes. The second part offers some additional resources that were very helpful to my thinking and might be valuable as you think about strangers and their place in your business and personal success. Taken together, these books, articles, and websites—mostly the work of people I've never met—have formed an essential part of the mix that became *The Necessity of Strangers*. You might say that I started with a large pot and a simple idea; threw in some water and a few stones; and then wandered around looking for ideas, insights, and perspectives from a world filled with strangers. As you might expect, these inspirations came from the usual places: business, psychology, and sociology, but also from the varied worlds of history, science, math, anthropology, nature, and even children's books and stories. In a very important way, our potential as individuals and organizations is influenced by our willingness to expand our world by reading, and by our openness to learning lessons from strangers—people, disciplines, and places beyond our usual reach.

Use these resources as a starting point for stretching your thinking or as a call to action to look in new places for ideas that could make a real difference to you and your organization. Then commit to the regular habit of picking up a book or ebook, reading a magazine or blog, or watching a movie or TV show that takes you off of your well-beaten path—not because everyone else around you is doing so, but because it might take you to a new and remarkable place where the possibility of a breakthrough awaits.

SUGGESTED READING

Acemoglu, Daron, James Robinson, and Thierry Verdier. "Can't We All Be More Like Scandinavians?" 2012. www.economics.mit. edu/files/8086.

Battutah, Ibn, and Tim Mackintosh-Smith, ed. *The Travels of Ibn Battutah*. London: Macmillan UK, 2003. Originally published in 1355 as *A Gift to Those Who Contemplate the Wonders of Cities and the Marvels of Travelling*.

Berger, Jonah. *Contagious: Why Things Catch On*. New York: Simon & Schuster, 2013.

Blau, Melinda, and Karen Fingerman. *Consequential Strangers: The Power of People Who Don't Seem to Matter . . . but Really Do*. New York: Norton, 2009.

Block, Peter. *Community: The Structure of Belonging*. San Francisco: Berrett-Koehler, 2008.

Burke, James. *Connections*. New York: Simon & Schuster, 1978.

Camus, Albert. *The Stranger*. New York: Knopf, 1988. Originally published in 1942.

Christensen, Clayton. *The Innovator's Dilemma*. New York: Harper Business, 2011.

Diaz, Alejandro, Max Magni, and Felix Poh. "From Oxcart to Wal-Mart: Four Keys to Reaching Emerging-Market Consumers." McKinsey

& Company, October 2012. http://www.mckinsey.com/insights/ winning_in_emerging_markets/from_oxcart_to_wal-mart_four _keys_to_reaching_emerging-market_consumers.

Dovodio, John. "On the Nature of Contemporary Prejudice: The Third Wave." *Journal of Social Issues* 57, no. 4 (2001): 829–849.

Duhigg, Charles. *The Power of Habit: Why We Do What We Do in Life and Business.* New York: Random House, 2012.

Ferrazzi, Keith, with Tahl Raz. *Never Eat Alone: And Other Secrets to Success, One Relationship at a Time.* New York: Currency Doubleday, 2005.

Gladwell, Malcolm. *The Tipping Point: How Little Things Can Make a Big Difference.* Boston: Little, Brown, 2000.

Haddon, Mark. *The Curious Incident of the Dog in the Night-Time.* New York: Vintage, 2004.

Harrison, K. David. *The Last Speakers: The Quest to Save the World's Most Endangered Languages.* Washington, DC: National Geographic, 2010.

Heinlein, Robert. *Stranger in a Strange Land.* New York: Putnam, 1963.

Holmes, Richard. *The Age of Wonder: How the Romantic Generation Discovered the Beauty and Terror of Science.* New York: Pantheon Books, 2008.

Hopgood, Mei-Ling. *How Eskimos Keep Their Babies Warm: And Other Adventures in Parenting.* Chapel Hill: Algonquin Books, 2012.

Johnson, Steven. *Where Good Ideas Come From.* New York: Riverhead, 2011.

John-Steiner, Vera. *Creative Collaboration.* New York: Oxford University Press, 2000.

Juster, Norton. *The Phantom Tollbooth.* New York: Knopf, 1961.

Kleon, Austin. *Steal Like an Artist: 10 Things Nobody Told You About Being Creative.* New York: Workman, 2012.

Kushner, Lawrence. *Invisible Lines of Connection: Sacred Stories of the Ordinary.* Woodstock, VT: Jewish Light, 2004.

Lehrer, Jonah. *Imagine: How Creativity Works*. Boston: Houghton Mifflin Harcourt, 2012.

Mayes, Frances. *Under the Tuscan Sun*. New York: Broadway Books, 1997.

Mayle, Peter. *A Year in Provence*. New York: Vintage Books, 1991.

Morgan, Michael Hamilton. *Lost History: The Enduring History of Muslim Scientists, Thinkers, and Artists*. Washington, DC: National Geographic, 2004.

Newberg, Andrew, and Mark Robert Waldman. *Born to Believe: God, Science, and the Origin of Ordinary and Extraordinary Beliefs*. New York: Free Press, 2006.

Ni, Maoshing. *Secrets of Longevity: Hundreds of Ways to Live to Be 100*. San Francisco: Chronicle Books, 2006.

Nisbett, Richard E. *The Geography of Thought: How Asians and Westerners Think Differently . . . and Why*. New York: Free Press, 2003.

Polo, Marco. *The Travels of Marco Polo, the Venetian*. Charleston, SC: Forgotten Books, 2012. Originally published in 1307.

Putnam, Robert. *Bowling Alone: The Collapse and Revival of American Community*. New York: Touchstone, 2001.

Reid Banks, Lynne. *The Indian in the Cupboard*. New York: HarperCollins, 1980.

Sawyer, Keith. *Group Genius: The Creative Power of Collaboration*. New York: Basic Books, 2007.

Sendak, Maurice. *Where the Wild Things Are*. New York: HarperCollins, 1963/1988.

Sims, Peter. *Little Bets: How Breakthrough Ideas Emerge from Small Discoveries*. New York: Free Press, 2011.

St. John, Warren. *Outcasts United: An American Town, a Refugee Team, and One Woman's Quest to Make a Difference*. New York: Spiegel & Grau, 2009.

Strogatz, Steven. *Sync: How Order Emerges from Chaos in the Universe, Nature and Daily Life*. New York: Hyperion Books, 2004.

Thompson, Clive. "Is the Tipping Point Toast?" *Fast Company*, February 1, 2008.

Tough, Paul. *How Children Succeed: Grit, Curiosity, and the Hidden Power of Character*. Boston: Houghton Mifflin Harcourt, 2012.

Wagner, Rodd, and Gale Muller. *Power of 2: How to Make the Most of Your Partnerships at Work and in Life*. New York: Gallup Press, 2009.

Watson, Peter. *Ideas: A History of Thought and Invention, from Fire to Freud*. New York: HarperCollins, 2005.

Weiss, Robert. *Learning from Strangers: The Art and Method of Qualitative Interview Studies*. New York: Free Press, 1994.

MAGAZINES

Science and innovation magazines—*Scientific American, Popular Science, Fast Company, Popular Mechanics, Discover, Wired, MIT Technology Review*

Travel magazines—*AFAR, National Geographic, National Geographic Traveler, Outside, Budget Travel, Travel & Leisure*

Special interest magazines—*Smithsonian, The New Yorker, Entertainment Weekly, Art News, Vogue, ESPN Magazine, Motor Trend, Magazine of Fantasy and Science Fiction, People*

NEWSLETTERS, BLOGS, AND WEBSITES

www.blogs.hbr.org

www.cleantechblog.com

www.customerthink.com

www.danpink.com

www.fastcompany.com

www.heathbrothers.com

www.innovationexcellence.com

www.kickstarter.com

www.kriscarr.com/blog

www.npr.org

www.pocketcultures.com

www.scienceblogs.com

www.sethgodin.com

www.ted.com

www.wired.com

NOTES

Chapter One: Necessity

1. Robin Dunbar, *How Many Friends Does One Person Need? Dunbar's Number and Other Evolutionary Quirks* (Cambridge: Harvard University Press, 2010).

2. Bill Bishop, *The Big Sort: Why the Clustering of Like-Minded America Is Tearing Us Apart* (New York: Houghton Mifflin, 2008).

3. Securities and Exchange Commission, September 20, 2004, filing by Blockbuster, Inc.

Chapter Two: Aversion

1. Wade Davis, *Light at the Edge of the World* (Vancouver: Douglas & McIntyre, 2007).

2. John Murray, "The Renewal of Antarctic Exploration," *Geographical Journal* 3, no. 1 (1894).

3. Roland Huntford, *The Last Place on Earth* (New York: Modern Library, 1999).

4. David Schilling, "Knowledge Doubling Every 12 Months, Soon to be Every 12 Hours," www.IndustryTap.com, April 25, 2013.

5. Anne Broache, "U.S. Won't Use Handhelds to Conduct Census," CNET, April 3, 2008.

6. Mahzarin Banaji and Curtis Hardin, "The Nature of Implicit Prejudice: Implications for Personal and Public Policy," in *The Behavioral*

Foundations of Public Policy, ed. Eldar Shafir (Princeton: Princeton University Press, 2013).

7. Katherine Boo, *Behind the Beautiful Forevers: Life, Death, and Hope in a Mumbai Undercity* (New York: Random House, 2012).

8. Isabel Fonseca, *Bury Me Standing: The Gypsies and Their Journey* (New York: Vintage Books, 1995).

9. Wade Davis, *The Wayfinders: Why Ancient Wisdom Matters in the Modern World* (Toronto: House of Anansi Press, 2009).

10. Human Genome Project, Final Report, April 2003.

11. William H. Whyte, "Groupthink," *Fortune,* 1952.

12. Irving L. Janis, *Victims of Groupthink* (New York: Houghton Mifflin, 1972).

13. National Commission on the BP Deepwater Horizon Oil Spill and Offshore Drilling, "Deep Water: The Gulf Disaster and the Future of Offshore Oil Drilling," Washington, DC, January 11, 2011.

14. Solomon Asch, "The Effects of Group Pressure on the Modification and Distortion of Judgements." In *Groups, Leadership and Men*, ed. H. Guetzkow (Pittsburgh: Carnegie Press, 1951).

15. John Bowlby, *Maternal Care and Mental Health* (World Health Organization, 1952). http://whqlibdoc.who.int/monograph/WHO_MONO_2_(part1).pdf.

16. Robert Burton, *On Being Certain: Believing You Are Right Even When You're Not* (New York: St. Martin's Griffin, 2008).

17. Ibid.

18. Christopher Chambris and Daniel Simons, *The Invisible Gorilla: And Other Ways Our Intuitions Deceive Us* (New York: Crown, 2010).

Chapter Three: Mindset

1. Victoria Cavaliere, "In Sardinia, World's Longest Living Family Credits Hard Work, Diet, Family," *New York Daily News*, August 23, 2012.

2. Michael Moss, *Salt Sugar Fat: How the Food Giants Hooked Us* (New York: Random House, 2013).

3. Carol Dweck, *Mindset: The New Psychology of Success* (New York: Ballantine Books, 2006), p. 6.

4. "The Mindsets." www.mindsetonline.com/whatisit/themindsets.

5. Ibid.

6. Ed Fuller, *You Can't Lead with Your Feet on the Desk* (Hoboken, NJ: Wiley, 2011).

Chapter Four: Innovation

1. "Vidal Sassoon Biography." www.thebiographychannel.co.uk.

2. Ibid.

3. See Mies van der Rohe Society, Chicago. www.miessociety.org.

4. Quoted in Bruce Weber, "Vidal Sassoon, Hairdresser and Trendsetter, Dies at 84," *New York Times*, May 9, 2012.

5. Walter Isaacson, *Steve Jobs* (New York: Simon & Schuster, 2011).

6. Nissan Motors, "Nissan EPORO Robot Car Goes to School on Collision-Free Driving by Mimicking Fish Behavior," news release, October 1, 2009.

7. Ibid.

8. Ibid.

9. Meaghan Haire, "A Brief History of the Walkman," *Time*, July 1, 2009.

10. Jacob Ganz and Joel Rose, "The MP3: A History of Innovation and Betrayal," NPR, *The Record*, March 23, 2011.

11. Jim Collins and Jerry I. Porras, *Built to Last: Successful Habits of Visionary Companies* (New York: Harper Business, 1994).

12. Brian Hindo, "At 3M, a Struggle Between Efficiency and Creativity," *Businessweek*, June 11, 2007.

Chapter Five: People

1. These quotes about the importance of people are taken from the following companies: General Electric, Goldman Sachs, Southwest Airlines, Price Waterhouse Coopers, Fred Meyer, USAIG, Decorline Interio, Exxon Mobil, PRG, Roche Roofing, Hasbro, Colorado Children's Hospital, Norfolk Southern.

2. Anya Kamenetz, "The Four-Year Career," *Fast Company*, February 2012.

3. Gene Weingarten, "Pearls Before Breakfast," *Washington Post*, April 8, 2007.

4. See Joshua Bell play in the metro station at www.youtube.com/watch?v=hnOPuo_YWhw.

5. Daniel Pink, *Drive: The Surprising Truth About What Motivates Us* (New York: Riverhead, 2009).

Chapter Six: Collaboration

1. James Krüss, "Mr. Singer's Nicknames," in *Junior Great Books, Series 4, Book 2* (Chicago: Great Books Foundation, 2006).

Chapter Seven: Customers

1. Joint Commission on Hospital Accreditation, "Top Performer on Key Quality Measures" Award, September 2011.

2. See the REI website at www.rei.com.

3. James Surowiecki, *The Wisdom of Crowds* (New York: Anchor Books, 2004).

4. To get a better sense of how crowdfunding works, check out www.kickstarter.com.

5. Salman Khan, *The One World School House: Education Reimagined* (New York: Twelve, 2012).

Chapter Eight: Leadership

1. Marcia Brown, *Stone Soup* (New York: Aladdin Picture Books, 1947/1997).

2. Michael Lewis, *Moneyball* (New York: Norton, 2011).

Chapter Nine: The Power of Travel

1. Maya Angelou, *Wouldn't Take Nothing for My Journey Now* (New York: Bantam, 1994).

Toolkit

1. Robert Kanigel, *The Man Who Knew Infinity: A Life of the Genius Ramanujan* (New York: Washington Square Press, 1992).

2. Duncan Watts, *Six Degrees: The Science of a Connected Age* (New York: Norton, 2004).

3. British Broadcasting Corporation, "Six Degrees of Separation," 2010. http://topdocumentaryfilms.com/six-degrees-of-separation/.

ACKNOWLEDGMENTS

While I am absolutely certain that strangers are a necessity in business and in life, I am equally certain that friends, colleagues, family, *and* strangers are a necessity in bringing a book to life—by providing fresh ideas, powerful insights, important questions, confused stares, laughter, premium quality chocolate, and a lot more encouragement than I probably deserve. Given this, let me try my best to thank many people who, whether they realize it or not, have been particularly helpful along the journey that became this book.

First, a thousand thanks to a wonderful group of friends, colleagues, and customers who continue to stretch my thinking about the nature of innovation and the real potential of people, companies, organizations, and especially strangers—including Sami AlBanna, Gunilla Almgren, Mary Amato, Stephanie Ambrose, David Anderson, C. E. Andrews, Ron Andro, Paul Anninos, Dennis Baker, Ibrahim Barghout, Kevin Beverly, Veer Bhartiya, Karen Blair, Barbara Bode, Mara Botman, Stuart Bowery, Steve Browne, Curtis Brunson, Brandon Busteed, Stephen Carroll, Ann Caton, Nancy Coleman, Chip Conley, Sherry Conway-Appel, Jerry Deatherage, Barbara DeLollis, John Dillon, Paul DiPiazza, Robby Dodd, Kendra

211

Ellison, Amr ElSawy, Marc Engel, Stefan Engeseth, Dave Epperson, Monica Escalante, Jan Fager, Cynthia Farrell-Johnson, Bill Flannery, Scott Fletcher, Laura Forman, Barbara Friedman, Teresa Fritsch, Yoshifumi Fukuzawa, Nicole Gadiel, Jody Giles, Ellen Glover, Aviva Goldfarb, Mary Good, Busy Graham, Addison Greenwood, Pam Gregory, Charlie Harmel, Ken Harris, John Hill, Perry Hooks, Jerry Hultin, Mike Jannini, Scott Jones, Stanley Kaplan, Sudhakar Kesavan, Myriam Khalifa, Shafiq Khan, Tim Kime, Kimo Kippen, Phil Kiracofe, Ved Krishna, Rudy Lamone, Peter Larsson, David Lent, Karen Lynskey, Ronny Maier, Manuel Mattke, Virginia Mayer, McArthur, John McKnight, Karen McSteen, Gil Miller, Esther Newman, John Northen, Tim Ogilvie, Hugh O'Neill, Ulgen Ozmen, Tom Paci, Dan Pink, Jim Parenti, Walt Plosila, Ian Portnoy, Jeremy Pound, Jeneanne Rae, Becky Ripley, Beverly Robertson, Jonathan Roos, Howard Ross, Larry Ross, Cynthia Rubenstein, Herb Rubenstein, Shyam Salona, George Schindler, Marie Schram, David Selden, Lee Self, George Selleck, Andy Shapiro, Harold Sides, Dan Simpkins, Erik Sorqvist, Pat Stocker, Scott Strehl, Matt Swayhoover, Mike Syracuse, Charbel Tagher, Tim Tobin, Leif Ulstrup, Ashish Vazirani, Dennis Whitelaw, Scott Wissman, Matthew Yalowitz, Eric Young, and Glenn Youngkin.

Second, sincere thanks to my agent, Giles Anderson, who found value in this topic from the start and challenged me to think differently about the best way to turn it into a meaningful book. To Karen Murphy, my editor at Jossey-Bass, who has been a thoughtful and enthusiastic partner in helping me to figure out exactly what I am trying to say without losing my voice—while gently reminding me that a sentence fragment by any name is still not a sentence, along with the entire team at Jossey-Bass for all of their help throughout the production and promotion process. And to Tom Neilssen and his colleagues at the BrightSight Group for their guidance and hard work in supporting my speaking activities.

And the biggest of thanks are due to my wonderful and intriguing family—especially my wife, Lisa, and our children, Sara, Carly, and Noah. You have always been in my corner, keeping dinner warm; helping me to stay focused; tolerating my jokes; reviewing my roughest drafts; listening to my semi-dramatic readings of several chapters; posting cool ideas and cooler pictures on flipcharts in my office; and understanding when I couldn't find time to help with homework, shoot baskets, walk Vincent (our kind and coward wonder dog), go to a movie, or play Apples to Apples and Banana-grams. I owe you all big-time. And I also want to thank my sisters, Sandy and Helene, with whom I continue to learn and laugh, and my parents—Norma and Ed Gregerman—who always encouraged me to look at the world with a sense of curiosity and openness. Although Mom is no longer with us, I still hear her voice encouraging me to connect with strangers from distant lands.

And last but not least, a final shout-out to all of the strangers whose lives, wisdom, and stories have shaped my understanding and sense of what is possible—folks who have crossed and shaped my path by design or chance.

ABOUT THE AUTHOR

Alan Gregerman is an award-winning author, business advisor, teacher, volunteer, and all-around nice guy. His writing and consulting work focuses on helping companies and organizations create winning strategies and more remarkable products, services, and customer experiences by unlocking the genius in all of their people. He also gives speeches and seminars, and leads "Team Learning Adventures" for corporations, associations, government agencies, colleges, and universities around the world. Alan is the author of two previous books, *Surrounded by Geniuses* and *Lessons from the Sandbox*, and his work and ideas have been featured on NPR, CNN, ABC News, and Fox News, and in *Businessweek*; the *Washington Post*, the *San Francisco Chronicle*, and more than 250 other publications. In his free time, he is founder and president of Passion for Learning, Inc., where he is involved in efforts to build innovative partnerships between the business community and low-income schools to close the achievement gap for at-risk children. He lives in the Washington, DC, area with his family.

To learn more and connect with Alan, please visit his blog at www.alangregerman.com.

INDEX

studying customer patterns
and interests, 138–140;
unlocking talent within
people, 85–87; using public
product reviews, 144–145;
valuing new hires, 93–95

C

Cayley, Sir George, 67
CEOs. *See* Leadership
Certainty, 37
Chambris, Christopher, 38
Closed mindsets, 45, 46, 47–49
Coddington, Grace, 70
Collaboration: designing work
for, 120–122; developing
relationships for, 113–116;
difficulties engaging
strangers in, 108–110;
encouraging employee, 74,
75; guidelines for, 112–116,
190–191; importance of, 8,
92–93, 107–108; mergers
and acquisitions as a,
127–130; questions leading
to, 122–126, 191–192;
sharing best thinking, 193;
technological means for,
110–111; tools for, 190–196
Community of strangers, 149–150
Conformity: groupthink and,
33–35, 94–95; tests of
individual, 35–36

Connecting. *See also*
Collaboration: with
customers, 140–141; finding
ways of, 118–120; with new
employees, 103–105
Context of ideas, 87–89
Cornu, Paul, 67
Crowdcube, 147
Crowdfunding, 147 148
Crowdsourcing, 144
Cubitron, 75
Curiosity, 51, 53–54
Customers: connecting with,
140–141; crowdsourcing
from, 144; developing new
ideas from, 145; reinventing
bond with, 131–134; role of,
131; starting social initiatives
among, 147–150; studying
buying patterns and
interests of, 138–140;
understanding strangers
who are, 134–138; writing
product reviews, 144–145

D

da Vinci, Leonardo, 67
Darwin, Charles, 131
Davis, Wade, 33
de Gerlache, Adrien, 23
de Launoy, Christian, 67
Deepwater Horizon disaster, 35
DemoHour, 147

11-13